Dr. Akhtar Hameed Khan – Pioneer of Microcredit & Guru of Rural Development

A Tribute on his 13th Death Anniversary

Collection of Articles & Poems

Author / Compiler:
Scholar and historian, Nasim Yousaf

Contributors:
Professor Norman Uphoff, Cornell University
Professor George H. Axinn, Michigan State
University
Akbar Khan, son of Dr. Khan

Published by:
AMZ Publications (USA)

Published by:
AMZ Publications
New York, USA

Table of Contents

Dedication

This work is dedicated to the legendary Dr. Akhtar Hameed Khan on his 13th death anniversary.

*****

Internet sites dedicated to respected Dr. A.H. Khan:

http://akhtar-hameed-khan.8m.com

https://www.facebook.com/dr.akhtarhameedkhan

Bangladesh (previously Pakistan) Academy for Rural Development:

http://www.bard.gov.bd

Orangi Pilot Project (OPP):

http://www.oppinstitutions.org

OPP – OCT:

http://www.oppoct-microcredit.com

Facebook pages:

https://www.facebook.com/Dr.AkhterHameed.Khan.founder.OPP

http://www.facebook.com/Dr.Akhtar.HameedKhan.Founder.BARD

Acknowledgements

I am grateful to distinguished Dr. Norman Uphoff, professor at Cornell University and former Director of Cornell International Institute for Food, Agriculture, and Development, and learned Professor Emeritus George H. Axinn of Michigan State University for their thoughtful contributions on Dr. Akhtar Hameed Khan. In addition, I would like to thank Akbar Khan, son of Dr. A.H. Khan, for the contribution of his eloquent poetry. I would also like to extend my cordial thanks to those learned persons, whose information I have used in my works.

Description of this Work

Dr. Akhtar Hameed Khan – Pioneer of Microcredit & Guru of Rural Development is a collection of ten articles and two poems on Dr. A.H. Khan – a world renowned social scientist and Nobel Peace Prize Nominee. Dr. Khan was a guru of rural development, pioneer of microfinance and recipient of many prestigious awards. He led the way in rural development and poverty alleviation. Dr. A.H. Khan was founder of two world-famous institutions, i.e. Bangladesh (previously Pakistan) Academy for Rural Development (BARD) and Orangi Pilot Project (OPP). Dr. Khan was also recognized by many academics, world leaders and global organizations, such as the World Bank, for his contributions to poverty alleviation. Dr. Khan passed away on October 09, 1999, and per his will, he was laid to rest on the premises of the OPP.

In honor of this great social scientist, his nephew, scholar and historian Nasim Yousaf, has published this work as a tribute to Dr. A.H. Khan on his 13th death anniversary. This compilation of pieces highlights Dr. Khan's work and achievements. This work contains articles authored by well-respected and illustrious scholars in their field and includes poems from an expert on rural development. The articles also include statements and views of a number of prominent and learned persons on Dr. Khan. These articles contribute to the enrichment of scholarship in the fields of microcredit, rural development, poverty alleviation and self-reliance based development.

The author and compiler, Nasim Yousaf, is a recognized historian and his works have been published globally in various mediums. Additional contributions have been included from the following distinguished persons: Professor Norman Uphoff of Cornell University, Professor Emeritus George H. Axinn of Michigan State University and Akbar Khan, son of Dr. Khan.

This work includes bios of the author and contributors as well as information on Dr. Khan's children. Sources, where available, are included within or at the end of each article.

About the Author / Compiler

Nasim Yousaf is a distinguished intellectual, scholar and historian. He has been in research since 1996. He is an out of the box thinker and is known for his bold statements and his open and courageous style of writing. He has traveled to many countries in Asia, Europe and North and South Americas.

The author comes from a famous and highly respected family of the Indian sub-continent. He is a grandson of Allama Mashriqi, whose book (*Tazkirah*, a commentary on the Holy Quran) was nominated for the Nobel Prize in Literature, and a nephew of Nobel Peace Prize Nominee Dr. Akhtar Hameed Khan.

Among all writers on Dr. A.H. Khan, scholar Nasim Yousaf is one of the few who have had the honor of knowing Dr. Khan firsthand. As his nephew, he had seen Dr. Khan in many different moments – during Dr. Khan's visit to the author's family house and at Dr. Khan's home in Comilla. Additionally, the author's knowledge comes directly from Dr. Khan's first wife (Hameedah Begum, a daughter of Allama Mashriqi) as well as sons and daughters of Dr. Khan and other relatives.

Nasim Yousaf has written extensively on Allama Mashriqi and Dr. Khan and topics related to the Indian subcontinent's history. His first book on Dr. A.H. Khan was published in 2003 under the title of *Allama Mashriqi & Dr. Akhtar Hameed Khan: Two Legends of Pakistan.* He has presented papers at U.S. conferences and published many books and numerous articles (which have appeared in newspapers of many countries, including Bangladesh, Canada, India, Japan, Norway, Pakistan, Sweden, United Kingdom, and the USA). He has contributed pieces to renowned journals and encyclopedias, namely *Harvard Asia Quarterly*, *Pakistaniaat* and *World History Encyclopedia* (21 Volumes published in 2011 by ABC-CLIO, USA).

Nasim Yousaf is currently working on additional articles and books, such as *World Famous Personalities in Microfinance and Poverty Alleviation: Nobel Prize Nominee Dr. Akhtar Hameed Khan, Nobel Prize Laureate Professor Muhammad Yunus and President Barack Obama's Mother, Dr. S. Ann Dunham* (tentative titles).

The author's family consists of his wife, son, son-in-law, and two daughters. His wife, Ambereen, works in a management position at large Fortune 500 corporation in U.S.A. The author's son, Zain, obtained his Bachelor's degree in Economics from Cornell University, MS in Management from Rensselaer Polytechnic Institute and MBA from New York University's Stern School of Business. His youngest daughter, Myra, is studying at Pennsylvania State University and is majoring in Political Science. The author's oldest daughter, Mehreen, obtained a BS in Industrial and Labor Relations from Cornell University, MS in Global Affairs from New York University and dual degree MBAs from London Business School and Columbia University Business School. His son-in-law, Hussain, married to his eldest daughter, attained a BS in Chemical Engineering from the University of Illinois at Urbana-Champaign and MBA from the University of Chicago's Booth School of Business.

For more information and updates on the author's works, visit:

www.allamamashraqi.com/grandsonsarticles.html

www.facebook.com/nasimyousaf.26

About the Additional Contributors

Dr. Norman Uphoff is a professor at Cornell University and former director of the Cornell International Institute for Food, Agriculture, and Development. He is an eminent professor and has various publications, including *The Political Economy of Development* (1972), *Local Institutional Development* (1986), *Reasons for Success: Learning from Instructive Experiences in Rural Development* (1997), and *Biological Approaches to Sustainable Soil System* (2006). He has been affiliated with many international organizations, such as USAID, World Bank and others. *The New York Times* paid rich tribute to him: "Many a professor dreams of revolution. But Norman T. Uphoff, working in a leafy corner of the Cornell University campus, is leading an inconspicuous one centered on solving the global food crisis. The secret, he says, is a new way of growing rice".1 He received his MPA from the Woodrow Wilson School of Public and International Affairs, and his PhD from the University of California at Berkeley.2

George H Axinn, Professor Emeritus, has had a longstanding and impressive history with Michigan State University, where he has taught for fifty years. His interests lie in international development, rural social systems, farming systems and other relevant areas. Over the years, he has helped establish MSU's reputation in his subject area, lived in various countries, and has been affiliated with many international organizations, e.g. Food and Agriculture Organization (FAO). He and his wife, Nancy Axinn, established the Department of Community, Agriculture, Recreation and Resource Studies (CARRS). They are distinguished scholar-practitioners committed to rural development. Their services are well regarded and in recognition for their contributions, in 2006, they were awarded the Distinguished Rural Sociologist Award by the Rural Sociology Society.3

Akbar Khan (born in Comilla), the only son of Dr. Khan, has worked for various organizations. From 1992-2000, he worked for Orangi Pilot Project (OPP) in Karachi (Pakistan) as the Director of the Rural Development Program. As OPP Director, he used to work with farmers at Glorachi village (200 kilometers from Karachi) and taught them how to increase the production of rice. With his efforts, farmers were able to increase the yield of rice from 26 units per acre to 66 units per acre in three years. Khan went to Faujdarhat Cadet College (Chittagong), then to Forman Christian College (Lahore) and thereafter, he went to Michigan State University and obtained a BSc. in Animal Husbandry.

For complete bios, visit the above personalities on the internet.

*****

Sources:

1 NY Times: published June 17, 2008
http://www.nytimes.com/2008/06/17/science/17rice.html?page wanted=all

2
http://www.cipa.cornell.edu/academics/corefaculty.cfm?person =19&letter=

3 http://africa.isp.msu.edu/faculty/bycollege.htm?id=6

http://www.carrs.msu.edu/programs/Axinn.php

About Dr. Khan's Family

Dr. Akhtar Hameed Khan (son of Khan Sahib Amir Ahmad Khan) was married to Hameedah Begum (daughter of Allama Mashriqi). After Hameedah Begum's death, Dr. A.H. Khan married Shafiq Khan.

Dr. Khan and Hameedah Begum's Children

a) Mariam is the eldest daughter of Dr. Akhtar Hameed Khan. After obtaining a Masters of Business Administration degree from Michigan State University in the USA, she worked as Director of Accounts at the Pakistan (now Bangladesh) Academy for Rural Development. Later, she joined the National Development Finance Corporation (Karachi). She was working as Senior Vice President, however she took early retirement. Her husband, Mehboob, held a senior position with an oil company.

b) Amina took on teaching as a profession and ran a private school in the USA. She is now retired. Her husband, Atiq, obtained a Masters Degree in Chemistry from the University of Karachi and later went to Stern Business School of New York University. From there, he completed a Masters of Business Administration. He retired as a Vice President and Head of a major region of a Fortune 500 corporation in the USA.

c) Rasheeda is an oncologist and works for a hospital in North America. Her husband, Amin, obtained a PhD in Engineering. Later, he went to a School of Medicine in Miami, Florida (USA). He stood first in his class. He was involved in the research on the balloon treatment of the heart. He passed away in Toronto (Canada).

d) Akbar, the only son of Dr. Khan, was born in Comilla, East Pakistan (now Bangladesh). He went to Faujdarhat Cadet College, Chittagong. He completed 12th grade from Forman Christian College, Lahore (Pakistan). Thereafter, he went to Michigan State University and obtained a BSc. degree in

Animal Husbandry in 1979. He worked for various organizations. However, from 1992-2000, he worked for Orangi Pilot Project (OPP) in Karachi (Pakistan) as the Director of the Rural Development Program. He used to work with farmers at Glorachi village (200 kilometers from Karachi) and taught them how to increase production of rice. With his efforts, farmers were able to increase the yield of rice from 26 units per acre to 66 units per acre in three years. After the death of his father, Akbar Khan moved to North America. He is married to Adeeba and they have a son, Zeeshan, who graduated from York University (Canada).

Dr. Khan and Shafiq Khan's (second wife after first wife passed away) Child

a) Ayesha (Dr. Khan's youngest daughter) is the only child of Dr. Khan with his second wife. She completed her studies at Aga Khan University Medical College, one of the top institutions in Pakistan, and is a physician. Ayesha is married to Adnan, also a physician. Both worked in the US for some time and then moved to Pakistan.

Collection of Articles & Poems

Dr. Akhtar Hameed Khan and President Barack Obama's Mother, Dr. S. Ann Dunham by Nasim Yousaf

A Tribute on Dr. Akhtar Hameed Khan's 12th Death Anniversary

*"In East Pakistan, Patten told me, he had worked with Akhtar Hameed Khan, an Indian born [Pakistani national], Cambridge educated social scientist and development activist, now recognized as a pioneer in what is known as microcredit"*1
— *A Singular Woman: The Untold Story of Barack Obama's Mother* by Janny Scott

World renowned social scientist Dr. Akhtar Hameed Khan (nominated for the Nobel Peace Prize2) was a pioneer of rural development, poverty alleviation and microcredit (extension of small loans to the poor). His ground-breaking methods have been applied around the world by everyone from Nobel Peace Prize Laureate Professor Muhammad Yunus to U.S. President Barack Obama's mother, Dr. Stanley Ann Dunham (who had a career in rural development and later promoted microcredit in Indonesia).

Dr. Khan first began experimenting with poverty alleviation in the mid-1940s. After resigning from the prestigious Indian Civil Service (I.C.S.), he, with his wife's (Nobel Prize Nominee in Literature Allama Mashriqi's daughter, Hameedah Begum) support, became a laborer and locksmith. Dr. Khan's new lifestyle served as a laboratory to test methods for combating poverty and changing the lives of the impoverished. Through this experience, Khan arrived at a novel conclusion: the destitute could be very productive if provided with some guidance and a small amount of working capital.

Dr. Khan would use this insight to develop two highly

innovative and successful projects: the Bangladesh (previously Pakistan) Academy for Rural Development (BARD) and the Orangi Pilot Project (OPP). Dr. Khan planted the seeds for BARD in 1950, when he came to Comilla (a poverty stricken area in the then East Pakistan) and began applying a new approach; instead of giving donations to the poor, he started a Karkhana (workshop) to help empower them; the method proved to be highly successful — an investment of only *Taka* (Bangladesh currency) 26.87 (approximately US $1.00) grew to $1.2 million (Source: *Small farm equipment for developing countries* by A.R. Bose).3 By the early 1960s, Khan had formally launched the Comilla Co-operatives at the said academy and introduced microcredit/microsavings, despite opposition from "moneylenders, whose income was cut substantially by the cooperative system and the increased productivity" (Scholar Ralph Smuckler).4 John M. Cohen (Professor at Cornell University and tenured Fellow of the Harvard Institute for International Development5) wrote of the highly successful initiative at Comilla, "In the history of international development, *Comilla*, or the Pakistan *Academy of Rural Development*, ranks as one of the most influential programs in the Third World..." 6

Dr. Khan's second monumental project was the now world-famous Orangi Pilot Project (OPP), which he established in Karachi (Pakistan) in 1980. The project was setup in Orangi Town, a low income settlement of over one million people, and its goal was to provide low cost sanitation, housing, health, education and small loans (microcredit) to the impoverished of the region. The project was again highly successful and received worldwide acclaim. The United Nations publication *Critical analysis of urban policies and their impact on urban poverty* later stated: "The Orangi Pilot Project (OPP) has evolved as one of the most successful NGOs both on national and international scale..."8

Dr. Khan thus emerged as a pioneer in the field of poverty alleviation and microfinance/microcredit; he received world recognition for his efforts, including a nomination for the Nobel Peace Prize. Indeed, Richard H. Patten (a brilliant

American economist), who had worked with Dr. Khan in the 1960s at the Bangladesh Academy for Rural Development (BARD) and had learned a great deal from Dr. Khan, described him as "the finest development worker I have ever met."9 As successful as his projects were, Dr. Khan's impact cannot be measured through his projects alone. His true genius lies in the replicable model that he introduced; following the success of his BARD and OPP projects, people from around the world began studying his methods and visiting his projects to learn from him and reproduce his success. In fact, most individuals are likely unaware that President Barack Obama's Mother, S. Ann Dunham (who worked in rural development) actually applied Dr. Khan's microcredit, poverty alleviation, and rural development schemes.

Like Dr. Khan, Dr. Dunham, an unpretentious and intelligent individual, worked with the poor and laid similar emphasis on craftsmanship, weaving and female empowerment. Over the years, Dr. Dunham worked with many of the same agencies as Dr. Khan, including the Ford Foundation, U.S. Agency for International Development (USAID), and the World Bank. There are also a number of examples that indicate that Dr. Dunham was inspired by Dr. Khan's work. For instance, in 1974, the Indonesian Government was seeking assistance in implementing microcredit and rural development schemes. The World Bank thus sent Dr. Khan to Indonesia (from February 10 to March 5, 197410) to survey the conditions and programs for rural development in Java (PARD 1974, 111). During his visit, Dr. Khan also spent time at many of the same sites where Dr. Dunham would later work, including Jakarta, Yogyakarta, Bogor, and Malang. Then, in January 1975, the East-West Center of the University of Hawaii (where Dr. Khan's works were well-known) invited Dr. Khan to read a paper.12 Here, Dr. Khan enlightened a large audience of his experiences at BARD. Dr. Dunham was also pursuing her studies at the East-West Center at the time. Later that same year,13 Dr. Dunham came to Indonesia to do anthropological field work in Java. Here, she would once again encounter Dr. Khan's work, as she would begin working closely with Richard Patten. Patten had worked with Dr. Khan at BARD (as referenced earlier) and was also with him during his trip to Indonesia, so he was quite familiar with Dr. Khan's projects (indeed Dr. Khan referred to Patten as his "old friend" in his report *Institutions for rural development in Indonesia*14). While working closely with Dr. Dunham in Indonesia, Patten shared Dr. Khan's ideas and methodology at BARD with her. Former *New York Times* reporter Janny Scott mentioned Dr. Khan and Patten in her book on Dr. Dunham (published in 2011) entitled *A Singular Woman: The Untold Story of Barack Obama's Mother*:

"In East Pakistan (now Bangladesh), [Richard] Patten told me, he had worked with Akhtar Hameed Khan, an Indian born [Pakistani national], Cambridge educated social scientist and development activist, now recognized as a pioneer in what is known as microcredit — the making of very small, or micro, loans to impoverished entrepreneurs. Khan, who had founded the Pakistan Academy for Rural Development, had been working on ways of lending money for small enterprises, including small shops. 'We followed what he had pioneered when we did a public works program in East Pakistan [now Bangladesh], Patten said. He was doing group credit through the cooperatives but then using a local bank to support it.' The Agency for International Development was interested in trying similar things in Central Java [Indonesia]." 15

Clearly, Dr. Khan had a major influence on Dr. Dunham's work. Ultimately, during her time in Indonesia, Dr. Dunham did marvelous work in poverty alleviation, rural development, microcredit, and women's empowerment.

Along with Dr. Dunham, Dr. Khan also inspired a number of other notable individuals in the field. In perhaps the most prominent example of the impact of Dr. Khan's work, among those who visited his Academy at Comilla was Professor Muhammad Yunus. Professor Yunus later established the famous Grameen Bank in Bangladesh in 1983, for which he won the Nobel Peace Prize.

It is certainly a testament to the mass movement in rural development initiated by Dr. Khan that people like Professor

Yunus and Dr. Dunham were able to successfully apply his methods. Even today, banks, NGOs, and microcredit and lending institutions continue to emerge from around the world following Dr. Khan's innovative example. Indeed, Dr. Khan's work has been admired by renowned individuals from both East and West. In addition to Dr. Dunham and Professor Yunus, Dr. Khan's admirers include Magsaysay Award (regarded as the Nobel Prize of Asia) winner Shoaib Sultan Khan and Former World Bank President Robert McNamara.16

Dr. Khan passed away on October 09, 1999. On his passing, the World Bank issued a statement (October 20, 1999):

"The World Bank and its country team for Pakistan are greatly saddened by the passing of Dr. Akhtar Hameed Khan last week. The World Bank holds Dr. Khan in great esteem for his groundbreaking work in poverty alleviation and raising standards of living through community participation..."

Indeed, the tributes to Dr. Khan continued to pour in long after his death. In a letter to me dated March 27, 2002, Micko Nishimizu (Vice President, South Asia Region, World Bank) graciously wrote of Dr. Khan:

*"...The life and work of this South Asian legend will continue to have repercussions far beyond the region, well into this millennium. His greatest legacy is the hundreds of disciples who continue his work in earnest, poised for victory in the battle against poverty."*17

And Former Vice Chancellor Jamia Millia Islamia (India) Syed Shahid Mahdi18 kindly wrote in an email to me on October 17, 2004:

"Dr. Akhtar Hameed Khan was unique figure of the subcontinent of the last century. His spirits of sacrifice and his untiring effort to ameliorate the condition of the disadvantaged should be a source of inspiration for us. Please accept my good wishes for keeping his memory alive".

Indeed, Dr. Khan, a simple and humble man, quietly changed the world. It is imperative that we continue to learn from him and apply his methods in order to confront the challenges faced by the impoverished today.

*****

1 Janny Scott, *A Singular Woman: The Untold Story of Barack Obama's Mother*, Publisher: Riverhead Books), p. 211.

2 Ralph Smuckler, *A University Turns to the World: A Personal History of the Michigan State University International Story*, p.112

3 A.R. Bose, *Small farm equipment for developing countries* by United States. Agency for International Development; International Rice Research Institute, p. 515.

4 Ralph Smuckler, *A University Turns to the World: A Personal History of the Michigan State University International Story*, p. 111.

5 John M. Cohen, *Integrated rural development: the Ethiopian experience and the Debate*, Publisher: The Scandinavian of African Studies, Uppsala, (February 1987), p. 02.

6 John M. Cohen, *Integrated rural development: the Ethiopian experience and the Debate*, Publisher: The Scandinavian of African Studies, Uppsala, (February 1987), p. 14.

7 *Morning News*, Dacca. Also see *The Easter Examiner* (Chittagong), September 01, 1963. *Pakistan Observer* (Dacca), August 14, 1963, *The Civil & Military Gazette* (Lahore), August 13, 1963

8 United Nations, *Critical analysis of urban policies and their impact on urban poverty*. Economic and Social Commission for Asia and the Pacific, p. 65.

9 Janny Scott, *A Singular Woman: The Untold Story of Barack Obama's Mother*, Publisher: Riverhead Books), p.278.

10 Akhtar Hameed Khan, *Report on Study Tour in Indonesia – 10th – 5th March 1974*, Pakistan Academy for Rural Development, Peshawar, Pakistan, 1974, p.1. Also see David L. Gordon, *Institutions for Rural Development in Indonesia* (Memorandum on Dr. Akhtar Hameed Khan's visit to Indonesia), Pakistan Academy for Rural Development, Peshawar, Pakistan, 1974, p.1 and

11 Ibid

12 Shoaib Sultan Khan, 1980, *Rural Development in Pakistan.* New Delhi, India: Vikas Publishing House Pvt. Ltd., p.153

13 Janny Scott, *A Singular Woman: The Untold Story of Barack Obama's Mother*, Publisher: Riverhead Books), p. 157.

14 Akhtar Hameed Khan, *Report on Study Tour in Indonesia – 10th – 5th March 1974*, Pakistan Academy for Rural Development, Peshawar, Pakistan, 1974, p.1

15 Janny Scott, *A Singular Woman: The Untold Story of Barack Obama's Mother*, Publisher Riverhead Books), p. 211.

16 *Allama Mashriqi & Dr. Akhtar Hameed Khan: Two Legends of Pakistan*, p. 351. Also see Akhtar Hameed Khan, 1985, Rural Development in Pakistan. Lahore, Pakistan: Vanguard Books Ltd., p. vi.

17 *Allama Mashriqi & Dr. Akhtar Hameed Khan: Two Legends of Pakistan*, p. 407-408.

18 He held many important positions, including serving as India's Alternate Permanent Representative to the Food and Agriculture Organization of the United Nations (FAO), Rome. Source: http://www.iansnews.com/jamia/en/aboutjamia/profile/history/

Past_Vice_Chancellors_Profile-
16/Mr_Syed_Shahid_Mahdi-2189

Dr. Akhtar Hameed Khan – An Inspirational Social Scientist by Nasim Yousaf

On His 11th Death Anniversary

"Of all the many outstanding personalities with whom I have worked abroad during the international program years at Michigan State [University], Akhtar Hameed Khan was the most impressive. He combined Gandhi-like sensitivity and dedication to the plight of the common man with the profound vision of a poet-philosopher; and he blended the considerable administrative skills of the elite Indian Civil Service (ICS) with the insights of an applied social scientist and historian1...His Scandinavian colleagues and other advisors had nominated him for the Nobel Peace Prize."2 — Scholar & Professor Ralph H. Smuckler.

Dr. Akhtar Hameed Khan was a pioneer in the disciplines of rural development and poverty alleviation as well as microfinance. According to Yasmeen Niaz Mohiuddin (Ralph Owen Distinguished Professor of Economics), his "'research and extension' methods of community development is followed today by numerous development agencies and NGO's around the world...His Comilla project is considered by many to be the precursor of world-renowned microfinance institutions."3 His contributions to rural development and poverty alleviation certainly rank him among the top social scientists of the twentieth century. But how did Dr. Khan grow to become a legend in the field and what lessons can be learned from his work?

Dr. Khan's early professional career was primarily in Government service. In 1936, he joined the Indian Civil Service (I.C.S.), a high status profession bestowed with virtually unlimited power by the colonial government. As an I.C.S. officer, Dr. Khan could have easily made a fortune for himself and attained a high social standing. However, he instead chose to pursue a life of public service. In 1959, the

Pakistan (now Bangladesh) Academy for Rural Development (BARD) was established at Comilla. It was here that Dr. Khan, as the Founding Director, launched his Comilla Cooperative scheme, which sought to uplift the impoverished through individual empowerment and grassroots involvement in the areas of agricultural and rural development. In implementing his program, Dr. Khan introduced a number of innovative methods for poverty alleviation, including microcredit, a novel concept predicated on providing small loans to the poor. His approach was not without opposition, however. When Dr. Khan first introduced his microcredit and microsavings schemes at BARD, a number of influential moneylenders opposed the scheme. Ralph Smuckler wrote in his book, *A University Turns To The World*, "…the Comilla Project did have serious enemies, among them the moneylenders, whose income was cut substantially by the cooperative system and the increased productivity." But Dr. Khan was determined to achieve his objectives, and ultimately his critics could not argue with the success of his methods. The Academy soon became a model for rural development, and other initiatives sought to replicate Dr. Khan's approach.

Witnessing Dr. Khan's outstanding work at Comilla, President Ayub Khan offered him the positions of Governorship of East Pakistan, Vice Chancellor of Dacca University, and Advisor to the President (Dr. Khan declined the positions). Additionally, Dr. Khan's work at Comilla earned him the admiration of the Bengali people. I personally witnessed the affection for Dr. Khan during my stay at his house in 1969. While there, I could sense the people's profound respect for him, as reflected by the photos of Dr. Khan in houses and shops throughout Comilla and other areas. The importance of Dr. Khan's pioneering work at Comilla continues to be recognized today. According to the book *Foreign Aid and Foreign Policy: Lessons for the Next Half-Century*, "The village small cooperative loan system set up through Comilla was a forerunner of the Grameen Bank, now considered a major breakthrough in terms microcredit."4 The current Joint Director of BARD, Milan Kanti Bhattacharje also wrote to me, "Dr. Khan is…often quoted here at BARD in different training courses, seminars, workshops and academic dialogues as the forerunner of micro credit." Additionally, he stated:

"The library of BARD is named as Akhter Hameed Khan Library...Comilla town fosters the memory of Dr Khan by naming one of its establishments as Dr. Akhter Hameed Khan Training Hall and another one as Dr. Akhter Hameed Khan Vocational Training Centre. Both are at the KTCCA [Kotwali Thana Central Cooperative Association] premises. The road connecting KTCCA Ltd., Comilla Export Processing Zone and some other important places of Comilla is named as Dr. Akhter Hameed Khan Sharak [Road]... some among the well-wishers of Khan established Dr. Akhter Hameed Khan Foundation... An old cottage at Comilla town also bearing memories of Khan is named as Akhter Hameed Khan Memorial House.

BARD, KTCCA and Foundation observe late Khan's birth and death anniversaries [anniversaries] and participate in each other's programmes...Khan's photos are displayed at several places at BARD premises...quotations from his writings/speeches at different corners, class rooms, conference rooms and library at the campus. KTCCA also does the same. Cooperative societies in many villages also display his photo and pieces of advice. BARD translated the three volumes of the Works of Akhter Hameed Khan *in Bangla...The Golden Jubilee publications of BARD contain some articles on Dr Khan. All these carry the sweet and inspiring memories of Dr Akhter Hameed Khan..."5*

Dr. Khan's success did not end with BARD. In 1980, he started another grassroots movement in Karachi under the name of the Orangi Pilot Project (OPP). Like BARD, it was established based on Dr. Khan's belief that self-help and self-reliance were key to development. According to Arif Hasan (writer and consultant to the United Nations), "Akhtar Hameed Khan established the OPP to develop sustainable models for the upgrading of low-income settlements, mobilizing local resources. He was a scientist and Orangi was his laboratory..."6 Once again, Dr. Khan's methods proved to be highly successful. Hasan further wrote in his book, "The OPP-

RTI programmes have made an impact at various levels. There is the impact in Orangi, in the OPP-RTI replication areas, on civil society and NGOs, on government projects and policies, on and donar-funded programmes, and on academia. The impact of the OPP-RTI programmes in Orangi has been stated in many publications."7 Dr. Khan's model at Orangi continues to be replicated not only in Pakistan, but in many parts of the world. A large number of visitors from within and outside the country regularly visit OPP to apply the lessons learned from Dr. Khan.

Through his decades of work on behalf of the impoverished, Dr. Khan made a tremendous impact. Deepa Narayan and Elena E. Glinskaya wrote in their book (published by the World Bank), "Over five decades, Dr. Akhter Hameed Khan, inspired and motivated thousands of development professionals in South Asia, winning a reputation as a visionary and teacher."8 Many prestigious honors — including the Sitara-i-Pakistan (1961), the Magsaysay Award (Asia's Nobel Prize, 1963), an Honorary Doctorate from Michigan State University (1964), and the Hilal-e-Imtiaz (2001) — were bestowed upon Dr. Khan in recognition of his unprecedented and pioneering work in rural development and poverty alleviation.

Dr. Khan passed away on October 9, 1999.9 Though he is no longer with us, his legacy lives on through his work. BARD and OPP applied techniques that were unprecedented in their time, and represent truly unique contributions from a Muslim social scientist to the world. They have become world-famous centers of excellence and have inspired prominent disciples, who continue to carry forward Dr. Khan's mission. For instance, Professor Muhammad Yunus, who applied microcredit at Grameen Bank, earned the Nobel Prize. Other notable disciples of Dr. Khan include Shoaib Sultan Khan (Magsaysay Award), Tasneem Ahmad Siddiqui (Magsaysay Award), Tahrunnesa Ahmed Abdullah (Magsaysay Award), and Mohammad Yeasin (Magsaysay Award). Thus, Dr. Akhtar Hameed Khan, the unsung hero of the East and West, quietly changed the world. For his unparalleled work and services to the nation, the Government of Pakistan should rename Orangi

Town (and the road leading to it) as Dr. Akhtar Hameed Khan Town. We must also continue to learn and spread Dr. Khan's methods, to inspire more great men like him.10 In this regard, it is imperative that his techniques of self-help development and poverty alleviation are included in the educational curriculum at all levels. In addition, research chair positions in various universities must be established to further explore and publish his groundbreaking methods, structures, and schemes. While Dr. Khan may have left us, such steps would help to ensure that his innovative methods for rural development, microcredit, and self-reliance continue to benefit the impoverished around the world for generations to come.

*****

1 *A University Turns To The World* by Ralph H. Smuckler, Publisher: Michigan State University Press (2003), p. 107. Ralph H. Smuckler, former Dean of International Studies and Programs and an acclaimed international scholar, led Michigan State University to worldwide recognition in the field of international education and public service.

2 *A University Turns To The World*, p. 112

3 *Pakistan: A Global Studies Handbook* by Yasmeen Niaz Mohiuddin, Publisher: ABC-CLIO, USA (2006), p. 305.

4 a) *Foreign Aid and Foreign Policy: Lessons for the Next Half-Century* by Louis A. Picard, Robert Groelsema, Terry F. Buss, Publisher: M.E. Sharpe (September 15, 2007), p. 310. M.E. Sharpe is a publisher of reference books, textbooks, journals in the social sciences and humanities, including titles in economics, management and public administration, history, and literature.

b) A. R. Bose writes, "The Comilla Cooperative Karkhana Ltd. is one of the oldest cooperative societies and the only of its kind in Bangladesh. Every regular employee is a shareholder and owner, and takes active part in production and management. The cooperative was established in 1950 by Dr. Akhter Hameed Khan, a social scientist, a founder of the Bangladesh Academy for Rural Development, and launcher of the Comilla-type cooperative for integrated rural development through cooperatives. After the partition of the Indian subcontinent in 1947, artisans who migrated to Bangladesh (then East Pakistan) sought Khan's help. Instead of giving financial help, Khan started the Karkhana (meaning workshop in Hindi and Bengali) with these refugees and some local landless people, with initial capital of only Taka 26.87 (approximately US$1.00)."

Source: *Small farm equipment for developing countries* sponsored by The United States Agency for International Development, The International Rice Research Institute (1986), p. 515. See heading "Organization and Development of the Comilla Cooperative Karkhana Ltd."

c) Rafael Ziegler stated, "It was not Yunus who created the idea of giving loans to the poor, and in this way help them to get out of their poverty. This idea was instead invented by Akhtar Hameed Khan. Yunus, however was driven, by a strong sense of mission to push this idea through." Source: *An Introduction to Social Entrepreneurship: Voices, Preconditions, Contexts* by Rafael Ziegler, Publisher: Edward Elgar Publishing (2009), p. 100-101.

d) Dr. Larry Dossey wrote, "The idea of microcredit in its current form was introduced in 1959 by Dr Akhter Hameed Khan, founder of the East Pakistan Academy for Rural Development." Dossey, Larry. Source: "The Peasant and the Professor: On Trust, Microcredit, and World Poverty," *Explore: The Journal of Science and Healing.*, Vol. 3, Issue 5, September 2007, p. 435.

e) Richard E. Boyatzis, PhD and Masud Khawaja, MD (Doctoral Student) also cited Dossey, writing, "As a result of the publicity that came with the Nobel prize, many people assume that Muhammad Yunus invented microcredit model for poor people. But the idea of microcredit, in its current form, was introduced in 1959 by Dr Akhtar Hameed Khan in the Comilla Project and then later used in the Orangi project." Source: "Resonant Leaders Leveraging Community and Country Sustained, Desired Change: The Case of the Amazing Dr. Akhtar Hameed Khan" by Boyatzis, Richard E. and Masud Khawaja. Paper presented at the Business as an Agent of World Benefit, 2009 Virtual Global Forum. (Richard E. Boyatzis, PhD Professor in Departments of Organizational Behavior, Psychology, and Cognitive Science, Case Western Reserve University, Cleveland, OH, USA. Masud Khawaja, MD Doctoral Student, Case Western Reserve University).

f) P. K. Bandyopadhyay writes, "The first micro-credit initiatives were introduced in Bangladesh with the Comilla efforts of the 1960s and later those of BRAC in Sylhet." Source: *The Bangladesh Dichotomy and Politicisation of Culture* by P. K. Bandyopadhyay, Publisher B.R. Pub. Corp. (2004), P. 57.

g) "Dr. Akhtar Hameed Khan is recognized as the creator of Microcredit, the idea was later picked up by Prof.Yunus and others." Source: http://www.designstudies.dsc.rmit.edu.au/index.php?Itemid=34 &catid=155&func=view&option=com_glossary&term=Microc redit

h) Dr. Faisal Bari writes, "The idea of micro-credit is not new to Pakistan either. In fact, one particular variant, acknowledged by Dr Yunus as well, has been in use in Pakistan from before the Grameen days. The Comila Pilot Project, started by the inimitable Dr Akhtar Hameed Khan, the founder of the Orangi Pilot Project in Karachi as well, experimented with ideas of self help, small loans and small projects on sustainable and viable basis a long time before Grameen was even formed. Dr Akhtar Hameed Khan's Orangi Pilot Project is a living tribute to his memory to date as well…" Source: *Dawn*, dated November 05, 2006, http://www.dawn.com/weekly/dmag/archive/061105/dmag1.ht m

i) "In 1960's Akhter Hamid Khan put into practice a 'modernising' project that reflected the aspirations of the post-colonial elite of Pakistan. His project is still continuing in full swing in Bangladesh." Source: *Seeds of Movements: On Women's Issues* in Bangladesh by Farida Akhter, Publisher: Narigrantha Prabartana (2007), p. 47.

5 Full quote:
"The library of BARD is named as Akhter Hameed Khan Library. You know Dr Khan established Kotwali Thana Central Cooperative Association Ltd. (KTCCA Ltd.) and led this organisation for several terms. KTCCA Ltd. near Comilla town fosters the memory of Dr Khan by naming one of its establishments as Dr. Akhter Hameed Khan Training Hall and another one as Dr. Akhter Hameed Khan Vocational Training Centre. Both are at the KTCCA premises. The road connecting KTCCA Ltd., Comilla Export Processing Zone and some other important places of Comilla is named as Dr. Akhter Hameed Khan Sharak. A few years back some among the well-wishers of Khan established Dr. Akhter Hameed Khan Foundation at Comilla town to keep alive Khan's memory and facilitate academic discussions on his philosophy and works. The foundation office is presently housed in Khan's once residence at Comilla town. An old cottage at Comilla town also bearing memories of Khan is named as Akhter Hameed Khan Memorial House. This is maintained by BARD.

BARD, KTCCA and Foundation observe late Khan's birth and death anniservaries and participate in each other's programmes. Every year BARD observes its birth anniversary (27 May) and organises Annual Planning Conference and records due regards to Khan on both the occasions. Khan's photos are displayed at several places at BARD premises. BARD displays posters bearing Khan's photo along with quotations from his writings/speeches at different corners, class rooms, conference rooms and library at the campus. KTCCA also does the same. Cooperative societies in many villages also display his photo and pieces of advice. BARD translated the three volumes of *the Works of Akhter Hameed Khan* in Bangla for wider publicity of his works, thoughts and ideals. The

Golden Jubilee publications of BARD contain some articles on Dr Khan. All these carry the sweet and inspiring memories of Dr Akhter Hameed Khan. Thank you again."
- Joint Director of Bard, Milan Kanti Bhattacharje

6 *Participatory Development - The Story of the Orangi Pilot Project-Research and Training Institute and Urban Resource Centre, Karachi, Pakistan* by Arif Hasan, Publisher: Oxford University Press (2010), p. xvii-xviii.

7 *Participatory Development - The Story of the Orangi Pilot Project-Research and Training Institute and Urban Resource Centre, Karachi, Pakistan* by Arif Hasan, Publisher: Oxford University Press (2010), p. 165.

8 *Ending Poverty in South Asia: Ideas That Work* By Deepa Narayan-Parker, Deepa Narayan, Elena E. Glinskaya, Publisher: World Bank Publications (November 15, 2006), p. 139.

9 Even after his death, the tributes to Dr. Khan continued. In Islamabad, a training and research institute was renamed as the Akhtar Hameed Khan National Centre for Rural Development and Municipal Administration (http://www.ncrd.gov.pk, 2000). Furthermore, the Council of Social Sciences (Pakistan) established an annual book award (Akhter Hameed Khan Memorial Award) in the name of Dr. Khan and the Jinnah Society honored him with the Jinnah Award (2004). Dr. Khan continues to be quoted in various seminars, discussion forums, and countless publications; a documentary has also been made about him.

10 Oxford University Press (Pakistan) has taken an initiative in this regard and published a book on Dr. Khan for children under the "Azeem [Great] Pakistani" series. The said publisher has also developed a syllabus (to assist teachers, academic coordinators and principals) entitled, "Model Curriculum Guide for Schools 2010" in which they have included Dr. Khan, so that Pakistani youngsters can learn from this great legendary man.

Remembering Dr. Akhtar Hameed Khan by Nasim Yousaf

On His 10th Death Anniversary

Dr. Akhtar Hameed Khan, social scientist, was born into a cultured and noble family on July 15, 1914 in Agra, India. He was the eldest son of Khan Sahib Amir Ahmad Khan. After completing his education in India, he joined the Indian Civil Service (I.C.S.). After joining the prestigious group of government servants, Dr. Khan went to Magdelene College at Cambridge University for two years, from 1936 to 1938.

In 1939, Dr. Khan married Hameedah Begum, the oldest daughter of the famous leader from South Asia, Allama Inayatullah Khan Al-Mashriqi. Their Nikah (Islamic marriage) ceremony was held at the end of 1939, and their Rukhsati (bride's departure from parent's home) was held in May 1940. After Hameedah's death, he re-married. From his first wife, he had three daughters and a son and from his second wife, he had a daughter.

Dr. Khan was the founder of the Pakistan Academy for Rural Development, Comilla (now known as Bangladesh Academy for Rural Development, BARD) and the Orangi Pilot Project (OPP), Karachi. The BARD was started in 1958 whereas the OPP was launched in 1980. Dr. Khan achieved global recognition as a result of his work on these exemplary community development projects.

In the early 1960's, Dr. Khan formally introduced microfinance / microcredit through the Comilla Co-operatives scheme (also known as Comilla Model or Comilla Approach); he demonstrated to the world that microfinance / microcredit models could work and could be applied on global scale. Today microcredit is a buzzword in the world of economic development and poverty alleviation.

Crediting Dr. Khan on microcredit, Louis A. Picard, Robert Groelsema, and Terry F. Buss wrote in their book entitled, *Foreign Aid and Foreign Policy: Lessons for the Next Half-Century*: "The village small cooperative loan system set up through Comilla was a forerunner of the Grameen Bank, now considered a major breakthrough in terms of microcredit."1

Microcapital Monitor (Massachusetts, USA) wrote in its issue of May 2008 under "Pioneers in Microfinance" (under written by Deutsche Bank): "...Khan is the originator of two development exemplars: the Comilla Model and the Orangi Pilot Project...Dr. Akhtar Hameed Khan helped lay the basic foundations of the microcredit movement through his work on the Comilla Model of rural development in the 1960s and the Orangi Pilot Project in the 1980s."2

Under the Comilla Co-operatives scheme, Dr. Khan also introduced microsavings. Initially the villagers could not grasp the concept, and Arthur F. Raper wrote of these villagers in his book: "'What does the man [Dr. Khan] mean — telling us [villagers] to save?'...'When we tell him we are too poor to save, he says that is why we must save.'" Raper went on to write in reference to said scheme: "The savings in the early days appear tiny indeed. During April, savings of the first seven agriculture societies ranged from Rs.12.00 to Rs. 65.00. The per-member monthly savings ranged from Rs.0. 60 (12 cents) to Rs. 2.65."3

Recognizing Dr. Khan's overall achievements at the Comilla Academy, the Board of Trustees of The Ramon Magsaysay Award Foundation (Philippines) honored him with the Magsaysay Award, also known as *Asia's Nobel Prize,* in August 1963. In 1964, Michigan State University awarded him with an Honorary Doctorate for his works and accomplishments.

Dr. Khan was also given many other awards for his innovative ideas, tremendous achievements, and contributions towards economic and human development. Among these were the Hilal-e-Pakistan, Sitra-i-Pakistan, Nishan-i-Imtiaz (posthumous), and Jinnah Award (posthumous).

Dr. Khan was also invited to speak at various forums and he shared his ideas at various institutions around the globe. Dr. Khan was a visiting professor at many distinguished universities, such as Harvard, Princeton, and Michigan State Universities in the USA, Lund University in Sweden, and Oxford University in England. Dr. Khan was also on the boards of various educational institutions in Pakistan.

Throughout the course of his lifetime, not only did he establish himself as a social scientist but also as a scholar and a poet. Dr. Khan possessed an immense amount of knowledge, and we could have learned much more from him, but his time came to depart. Dr. Khan left us on October 09, 1999; he died in the USA where he was visiting his family.

Today, Dr. Khan's ideas and works are quoted in books and journals and are not only globally recognized but replicated in various countries of the world. Millions of unprivileged people are benefiting from these projects in Pakistan, in Bangladesh, and across the globe.

May Dr. Akhtar Hameed Khan rest in peace and may God bless his soul.

*****

1 Picard, Louis A., Robert Groelsema, and Terry F. Buss. *Foreign Aid and Foreign Policy: Lessons for the Next Half-Century.* M.E. Sharpe, 2007. p. 310.

2 "Pioneers in Microfinance: Dr. Akhtar Hameed Khan." *MicroCapital Monitor.* Volume 3, Issue 5. May 2008. http://www.microcapital.org/downloads/monitor_volume3/MicroCapitalMonitorPreview_May08.pdf

3 Raper, Arthur F. *Rural Development in Action: The*

Comprehensive Experiment at Comilla, East Pakistan (now Bangladesh). Cornell University Press, 1970. pp. 66-7.

Dr. Akhtar Hameed Khan's Vision of Development through Self-Reliance by Nasim Yousaf

On Dr. Khan's 9th Death Anniversary

Introduction

"Give a man a fish and you feed him for a day. Teach a man to fish and you feed him for a lifetime." Acclaimed social scientist Dr. Akhtar Hameed Khan used to reference this well-known proverb (according to his son, Akbar Khan), as it quite fittingly represents his philosophy on community development. To Dr. Khan, the solution to Pakistan's problems did not lie in giving free charity, but rather in *teaching* people the methods of development, so that they could stand on their own two feet. Dr. Khan's belief in this philosophy is clearly evident through his works, including the Orangi Pilot Project (OPP), a non-governmental organization (NGO or CBO [Community Based Organization]) that focused on self-reliance to improve the lives of the residents of Orangi Town in Karachi, Pakistan.

Background

In Pakistan, a Katchi Abadi refers to a public settlement that is not recognized by the government for a development program or other assistance. According to Dr. Khan, a Katchi Abadi had five inherent problems: housing, sanitation, health, education and employment. The town of Orangi was a prime example of a densely populated Katchi Abadi; it was completely neglected by the Government, and lacked any formal development projects to improve the quality of life of the residents. As a result, the residents were forced to endure a filth-ridden environment lacking a sewerage system, electricity, and other basic amenities. The prevailing conditions translated into a high illness and death rate among the community. Without Government support, the conditions at Orangi remained at a standstill – that is, until the introduction of Dr. Khan's Orangi Pilot Project in 1980. More specifically, two aspects of the project in particular provide especially fitting examples of Dr. Khan's emphasis on self-reliance: (1) the development of a sanitation system by the residents of Orangi and (2) the use of microcredit.

Development of a Sanitation System

As aforementioned, Orangi was littered with filth and the residents lived in the most unhygienic conditions. A major underlying cause of this situation was the lack of an adequate sanitation system – a byproduct of the residents' meager resources and the lack of Government support. Dr. Khan described the problem in the *Pakistan & Gulf Economist* (June 11-17, 1983) in a special report on the Orangi Project:

"A man who has spent Rs. 15,000 or Rs. 20,000 on building his house…cannot pay Rs. 10,000 for the drainage…Though it is so shameful to relate but it is not a secret that for every hundred rupees charged by the contractor about 20 to 30 per cent is kickback. The contractor himself was not ashamed of admitting that he was charging 40 to 50 percent profit…"

Dr. Khan recognized that there was a problem, but he also knew that it was important to understand the underlying issue before arriving at a solution. According to Dr. Khan's son, Dr. Khan used to say, "never start a program with a blueprint in mind." A careful survey of the situation led Dr. Khan to the conclusion that Orangi's sanitation problem could not be improved without a strong emphasis on self-reliance.

Thus, Dr. Khan sought to empower the residents of Orangi to build their own sanitation system – without aid from the Government or from domestic or international donor agencies. Based on an overarching philosophy of self-reliance, he worked with the residents of Orangi to formalize a plan for their sanitation system. The residents would have to purchase materials from their own pockets to build the sanitation system, and would be required to work on the project without outside charity. Meanwhile, the OPP would provide free technical assistance. Dr. Khan wrote in the *Pakistan & Gulf Economist* (June 11-17, 1983), "The ignorance of the people about the technology of the sewerage system was removed by undertaking teaching programmes." Dr. Khan ensured that the entire initiative was undertaken ethically and with the utmost sense of transparency. For instance, residents would have the liberty to buy materials from a source of their choice, in order to ensure that the OPP would not be accused of taking commission from a recommended shop.

The sanitation project at Orangi proved to be a tremendous success. Through their collective efforts, the residents of Orangi were able to build a modern sewerage system for the town. Aside from the health benefits of the new system, the process of building the system proved to be a valuable activity in itself. The residents learned how to problem solve and work collectively to achieve common goals. They were also able to pass on the techniques they learned to others. And the project was completed ethically, without corruption. For the country, the initiative at Orangi saved money for the government exchequer, as it developed the community inexpensively, free from costly foreign loans or foreign experts. Perhaps the most important benefit of the development of the sanitation system at Orangi was that it proved to the world that impoverished communities could be developed on a self-help basis.

Microcredit at Orangi

Like the development of the sanitation system, the application of microcredit at Orangi is another example of Dr. Khan's firm belief in self-reliance. Dr. Khan had originally applied microcredit at the Comilla Co-operatives at the Pakistan Academy for Rural Development (PARD) (now Bangladesh Academy for Rural Development – the successful application of microcredit at Comilla led to its adoption by Nobel Prize winner Professor Mohammad Yunus and others).

Based on the success of microcredit at Comilla, Dr. Khan launched a similar scheme at OPP. He established the OPP-

Orangi Charitable Trust (OCT) to provide residents with small loans for running micro-enterprises of their choice. For example, a resident could borrow funds to open a tailoring shop or to sell arts and crafts. Microcredit enabled those who were unemployed to become self-employed, and thereby transformed them into active contributors in the country's economy. It also reaffirmed the concept of self reliance in order for the residents to improve their lives.

The microcredit concept was well received at Orangi, and its success is evident even today. In fact, 70% of the 1.2 million residents of Orangi Town are self-employed. Furthermore, the recovery rate on loaned funds remains strong at 95% (http://www.oppoct-microcredit.com/Process%20of%20Loan.htm).

Dr. Khan's microcredit scheme has been praised globally. MicroCapital Monitor, a journal from Massachusetts (USA), wrote in its May 2008 issue (dated May 2008, Volume 3 Issue 5) under the title *Pioneers in Microfinance*: *Dr. Akhtar Hameed Khan* (a series sponsored by Deutsche Bank), "Dr. Akhtar Hameed Khan helped lay the basic foundations of the microcredit movement through his work on the Comilla Model of rural development in the 1960s and the Orangi Pilot Project in the 1980s."

Thus, through the concept of microcredit, Dr. Khan once again successfully harnessed the concept of self-reliance to help the residents' of Orangi improve their lives and also to set an example for others to follow.

Conclusion

From the very beginning, the OPP has worked without Government or foreign aid, loans or foreign advisors. The initiative has completely relied on local resources and manpower. Based on the success of the OPP, domestic and international experts (including students from various universities around the world) began to visit the OPP. The institution has thus transformed into a learning and development center for undertaking projects on a self-help basis. Papers the world-over continue to be written on the OPP. Its success can be further gauged from the fact that the OPP Model is being replicated not only in Pakistan, but throughout many parts of the world, including Sri Lanka, India, Nepal, South Africa, and Central Asia (*Dawn* October 13, 1999). Furthermore, the rise of microfinance and microcredit techniques has led to the creation of a large number of Non-Governmental Organizations (NGO), foundations, and journals focusing on the subject.

The tremendous success of the "Development through Self-reliance" model would not have been possible without the visionary leadership of Dr. Akhtar Hameed Khan. Taken in isolation, Dr. Khan's work at Orangi is a *remarkable* achievement. However, when considering its impact on other development efforts around the world, it becomes a *revolutionary* achievement. Though Dr. Khan passed away in October of 1999, he has left behind a legacy of new concepts, ideas, and admirers the world over. In an article on October 22, 2000, Indian daily newspaper *The Hindu* wrote, "Just who would you vote for as the greatest Gandhian in the Indian sub-continent in the post-Independence period? Our vote will unhesitatingly go to the Pakistani social scientist Akhtar Hameed Khan...[his] death is a loss not just for Pakistan but for everyone in the subcontinent. But like Gandhi he will remain immortal because of the inevitability of his ideas." During a keynote address on June 21, 2008 at the annual Dr. Akhter Hameed Khan Memorial Lecture, K. Raju (Principal Secretary to the Rural Development Department, Government of Andhra Pradesh Hyderabad) stated that Dr Khan "deeply influenced the development discourse not only in this country but in several others, including my own country, India...we believe that Khansaheb was the greatest Gandhian of the entire sub-continent in the post independence period" (http://www.irm.edu.pk/ahkrcnew/Annual_Memorial_lecture_2 008.asp).

In closing, it is important to note that Dr. Khan's accomplishments are Pakistan's accomplishments as well - as a

Pakistani citizen, he is widely recognized for benefiting the lives of millions around the world. And although this social scientist and reformer has passed away, the spirit of self-reliance and community-based development that he inspired shall live on forever.

Dr. Akhter Hameed Khan – The Pioneer of Microcredit by Nasim Yousaf

On Dr. Khan's 8th Death Anniversary

It's hard to believe that microcredit - which has exploded into the world of finance in recent years - was considered an unfeasible concept at one time. Microcredit provides very small loans to those who have no verifiable credit history or collateral that would be acceptable to a financial institution. Prior to the microcredit methodology, banks served only the privileged and, as a result, perpetuated the gap between the poor and the rich. However, in the 1950s and '60s, Dr. Akhter Hameed Khan, a world-renowned social scientist from Pakistan, initiated the Comilla cooperative program, and proved to the world that it was indeed possible to provide credit to the poor – with great success no less.

In order to gain a greater understanding of why Dr. Khan's cooperative scheme was so successful, one needs to travel back to the 1950s - the early years of the Pakistani nation. Since its founding in 1947, the country as a whole had been plagued by a number of problems, primarily related to administration and infrastructure, lack of industrialization, poor communication, a large population, unemployment, and poverty. The challenges at the national level also translated into individual components of the economy. Problems in the agriculture sector were particularly severe — they included disorganized farming, poor yield (despite favorable conditions), crop damages from floods and pests,1 lack of application of modern techniques, no guidance or training, and improper marketing. Furthermore, small farmers' land holdings in the villages (in East Pakistan) ranged from one to five acres and they were in a miserable condition.2 According to Dr. Khan, "Ninety percent of them owned less than five acres."3 Needless to say, the prevailing environment made it very difficult for those who relied on agriculture for their livelihood. But how had these conditions come about? Therein lies perhaps the greatest challenge of all faced by the small farmers: lack of access to a credit facility.

Poor farmers in Pakistan had no creditworthy history or collateral that would be acceptable to banks and other financial institutions. Thus, the financial institutions were unwilling to risk their money by granting loans to the poor farmers. This meant that farmers were at the mercy of private lenders, traders, etc. The lenders leveraged their advantageous position to charge high interest rates and earn profits at the expense of the working poor. According to Dr. Khan, "They [farmers] were short of capital, and in their distress, borrowed from exorbitant money lenders, and sold to oppressive traders. Small scale agriculture, starved of capital, and skill, damaged by risks, and squeezed by high interest rates and low prices for their output, was in fact going bankrupt."4 Under such conditions, the impoverished were left with no incentive to learn and adopt modern techniques or increase their per acre agricultural yield.

In an attempt to address these problems, the Government of Pakistan established the Pakistan Academy of Rural Development (PARD). In 1958, Dr. Khan was appointed as Director of the newly formed organization,5 and the Academy began functioning in May of 1959.6 Upon taking the helm, Dr. Khan was confronted with the serious problems facing the agriculture sector. He traveled from village to village to conduct research, gain a more intimate knowledge of the farmers' troubles, and discuss their issues; his focus was on *listening*, rather than dictating.

Speaking with the villagers, Dr. Khan quickly recognized that ensuring collaboration between the farmers would be key to relieving many of their ailments; he determined that a cooperative system would be the best means to enable this collaboration. Such a system would allow farmers to share information, make joint production decisions, and leverage their collective resources to establish a basis for credit-worthiness, thereby reaping mutual benefits. In designing the system, Dr. Khan emphasized the broad principles of "savings, educational meetings, joint planning and action."7

But Dr. Khan knew that no cooperation would be possible without the backing of the villagers. Thus, efforts were undertaken to travel to the different villages to espouse the benefits of the system and gain support from the villagers. As a result of Dr. Khan's efforts, the villagers began to organize and the cooperative experiment at Comilla was underway.

By May of 1960, ten local cooperatives had been organized. According to author Arthur F. Raper in his book *Rural Development in Action: The Comprehensive Experiment at Comilla, East Pakistan*, these ten cooperatives were comprised of "seven village-based agricultural societies, a vegetable growers' society, a women's cooperative, and a weavers' cooperative."8 Raper further states that by 1961 "17 village societies had...secured 25 loans totaling Rs. 108,000. The largest amount borrowed by any village society [cooperative] was Rs. 15,000 and the smallest Rs. 2,500. These loans were arranged through either the Comilla Cooperative Bank or the Agricultural Bank at Comilla."9

As the Comilla experiment matured, there was recognition that a central association was needed to support the local cooperatives (also known as primary cooperatives). So, in January of 1962, the Kotwali Thana Central Cooperative Association (KTCCA) was registered, with Dr. Khan as Chairman of its managing committee.10 Thus, a two-tier system - comprised of the cooperatives of small farmers at the local village level and a centralized supporting association at the thana level – emerged.11

Here it is important to explain the respective roles of the primary cooperative and the central association in the two-tier system. The primary cooperative consisted of a group of farmers from a given village (or sometimes multiple villages). In order to participate in the Academy's cooperative program, they had to meet certain requirements, including:

-Holding regular meetings with mandatory attendance by all member villagers. 12

-Electing a representative/manager.13 Each representative manager was required to connect with the central association weekly, not only to obtain training but to deliver any messages back and forth. The manager communicated on all issues, including credit. His responsibilities also included holding training classes in his respective village and disseminating knowledge which was imparted to him by the central association.

-Collecting regular savings deposits from its members. The manager of the primary cooperative then deposited the savings with the central association.14 It is important to note that these deposits were a key tenet of the cooperative system, as they would help to build savings in the local communities, and also provide capital for subsequent loans.

As aforementioned, the central association provided support to the primary cooperatives.

In the case of the KTCCA, its services included: 15

-Training and education

-A Service Center to procure, rent and repair farming machinery

-Banking (capital accumulation, credit, commercial marketing)

-Teaching scientific methods

The KTCCA derived its funds from private as well as public sources, including the Government, the Ford Foundation, and the primary cooperatives. Using these funds, it was able to offer loans to the primary cooperatives, who in turn provided credit to their members. In essence, the Comilla Cooperative had established its own banking system, which, for the first time, allowed small farmers to obtain loans at low interest rates.16 Furthermore, it enabled farmers to learn and adopt modern techniques. As a result, both the individual household and the country benefited.17

Indeed, the Comilla Cooperative had proven to be a tremendous success; the movement started by Dr. Khan was no less than a revolution! The system worked because (according to A. Aziz Khan in *Comilla Co-operative Pilot Project [1961-1965]*) "on the one hand, they [village societies] have the strength of proximity, homogeneity, mutuality of knowledge and vigilance among their members and on the other they have the necessary support from the Central Association."18 Perhaps Dr. Khan himself best summarized the reasons behind the success of the Comilla program:

"The Comilla project proposed a way out of the dilemma of the small village cooperative being economically weak, and the multi-village cooperative lacking in social and psychological cohesion, by establishing a large number of primary groups based on single villages, and federating them into a powerful central association. Each strengthens and sustains the other. Each performs well defined task and function. In combination, the primary village groups and their federation, form the nucleus of a new economic order for rural areas."19

In the years subsequent to the founding of the Comilla Cooperative, a number of other initiatives were launched to replicate the success seen at Comilla. Nonagricultural societies – modeled after the Comilla Cooperatives - were formed in East Pakistan (now Bangladesh) and operated under the Special Cooperative Societies Federation (SCSF).20 These societies represented such diverse occupations as rickshaw pullers, merchants, butchers, weavers, village doctors, blacksmiths, factory workers, motor drivers, etc.21 By the middle of 1968, there were 261 agricultural societies and 78 societies in the Special Cooperative Societies Federation.22 Meanwhile, in Bangladesh, Professor Muhammad Yunus was closely observing the success of microcredit at the Comilla cooperatives, and in 1983 started Grameen Bank; he won the 2006 Nobel Peace Prize for his application of microcredit there. In 1989, the Orangi Pilot Project - Orangi Charitable Trust (OPP– OCT) was established in Karachi, Pakistan by Dr.

Khan as an independent institution to provide microcredit in urban and rural areas. In yet another example, in August of 2000, Khushali Bank was formed in Pakistan to provide microcredit. Today, the concept of microcredit is being applied in many countries around the world, thanks in large part to Dr. Khan's efforts at Comilla.

Thus, through his pioneering work at the Comilla Cooperative, Dr. Akhter Hameed Khan brought the idea of microcredit to the world stage. Dr. Khan's work has opened doors for the impoverished, while simultaneously erasing misconceptions and stereotypes. He has proven to the world that the poor can be effective participants in the economy if given the opportunity. Dr. Khan's contributions to rural development, poverty alleviation, and the microcredit scheme will surely live on forever.

*****

Many experts and learned men, including the President and Prime Minister of Pakistan, have acknowledged Dr. Khan's incredible accomplishments. Below are a few excerpts:

General Pervez Musharraf, President of Pakistan (during an interview):

"...he [Dr. Khan] introduced health, poverty alleviation, education projects which were so welcomed, and he did it by being with the people, living with them. I think he was one of the great figures of the region of South Asia...He was a man for the people, and we need such personalities as Akhter Hameed Khan..."23

Shaukat Aziz, Prime Minister of Pakistan (then Federal Minister for Finance, Pakistan, speaking at an Agha Khan Rural Support Programme [AKRSP] conference):

"Ladies and Gentlemen! We are proud that the AKRSP model is totally 'homegrown'. It is an iteration of the ideas and experiments of the great visionary and teacher, Dr. Akhtar

Hameed Khan."24

Professor Muhammad Yunus, 2006 Nobel Peace Prize winner and admirer of Dr. Khan (in his letter sent on the occasion of a symposium on the Life and Times of Dr. Khan, held in Islamabad from March 02-05, 2000):

"He [Dr. Khan] was one of the greatest human beings of the past century. He was so much ahead of everybody else that he was seen more as a 'misfit' than appreciated for his greatness. Dr. Khan needs to be rediscovered in the light of the realities and needs of the emerging century. We have a lot to discover and a whole lot to learn from him."25

Shoaib Sultan Khan, Chairman of the National Rural Support Programme (NRSP):

"He was my mentor not only in name but in reality. Every time I met him, I learnt something new...

He never failed me in showing the light when I would be desperate and have the feeling of being caught in a cul de sac or faced with an insurmountable wall. He would explain every issue--social, economic, temporal or metaphysical--with the ease of a person having full command on the subject. His explanation of the religions of the world especially of Islam used to have a depth and breadth which left even the most ignorant deeply moved."26

W. Klatt, St. Antony's College, University of Oxford (in a book review of *Rural Development in Action: The Comprehensive Experiment in Comilla, East Pakistan* by Arthur F. Raper):

"The man responsible for this [women's participation and development] and other changes in attitude is Akhter Hameed Khan, at one time a member of the I.C.S., after 1959 the Academy's director, and recently appointed Vice-Chairman of its Board of Directors...He is indeed a remarkable man without whom the Academy would not be worth writing about...

The experiment's main success lies in the village co-operatives, the pubic works program and the women's share in changing life in the villages."27

David E. Bell, Vice President, The Ford Foundation:

"The Comilla story centers in a more important sense around a man — a remarkable man — Akhter Hameed Khan...[who] is the prime cause of its [the Academy's] success...

The choice [of Dr. Khan] could not have been wiser, for it was he who brought to the Academy its central concept..."28

Harvey M. Choldin, Michigan State University:

"There is no denying that Akhter Hameed Khan, the first director of the academy, has been the centrally important figure within the programs there...He has developed a reputation for concern for East Pakistani problems over a period of decades, as a high civil servant working in that area and as the head of a local college. Within the government, he has access to high civil servants, some of whom were colleagues of his in the Indian Civil Service before independence...His style combines erudition with humility and simplicity. He works long hours, with, at times, a great deal of contact with village people, often through the medium of long walking tours through the villages."29

Harvey M. Choldin (in another article):

"Many observers consider these projects [at Comilla] to be among the most successful rural development efforts in underdeveloped areas. The projects offer an opportunity for social scientists to observe and analyze modernization processes..."30

Harry W. Blair (in *Pacific Affairs* journal):

"The Pakistan Academy for Rural Development at Comilla,

East Pakistan, has been widely considered as an outstanding example of a successful community development program. Under the leadership of its director, Akhter Hameed Khan, the Academy has had an especially impressive record of achievement in its major activity of establishing cooperative development projects. Its program revolves primarily around three spheres of activity: agricultural credit, the provision of training and supplies, and research."31

Dr. Ishrat Hussain (while he was at the World Bank):

"...Today micro-credit has become a buzzword in the lexicon of development practitioners for poverty alleviation throughout the world but 35 years ago this idea was pioneered in Comilla."32

Dr. Norman Uphoff, Cornell University:

"Sadly, such towering figures and lofty intellects as Akhter Hameed's are quite uncommon. Only a few emerge in any generation. His lifetime spanned an era of incredible change, with remarkable advances in certain political and economic respects, and lamentable failings in these same realms."33

Professor Rehman Sobhan, Chairman, Centre for Policy Dialogue, Dhaka, Bangladesh (as part of a lecture on "Democratizing Development in South Asia: Responding to the Challenge of Globalization," which he was delivering upon the invitation of the Akhter Hameed Khan Resource Center in association with the Rural Support Programmes Network):

"Akhter Hameed Khan was an inspiration to my generation. I had the privilege of learning from him when I was a young teacher of economics at Dhaka University in the early 1960s. His model of rural development was then making its impact in Comilla Thana and its headquarters in the Abhoy Ashram in Comilla had already became a place of pilgrimage for those at home and from abroad seeking inspiration for resolving the problems of poverty in an increasingly unequal society. What lent credibility to Akhter Hameed sabib's endeavours was his

own human personality and willingness to realign his career choices to conform to his beliefs. The simplicity of his manner, the austerity of his life style, the wry, selfdeprecating humour with which he dealt with people of all classes, age groups and background served as a testament to his commitment and integrity as a human being...

The ultimate tribute to Akhter Hameed's contribution to changing the lives of the less privileged are to be found in the role models he inspired. In Bangladesh people such as Mohammed Yunus, founder of Grameen Bank and our most recent Nobel Laureate, targeted the landless groups as the principal beneficiary of collateral free micro-credit."34

Professor Emeritus George H. Axinn, Michigan State University:

"In my mind and heart, the greatest professional and human contribution to rural development in the second half of the 20th Century was made by Akhter Hameed Khan." 35

*****

1 *Personal Reminiscences of Change* by Akhter Hameed Khan, Publisher United Nations Children's Fund (UNICEF), March 1994, p. 2.

2 *The Works of Akhter Hameed Khan, Vol II Rural Development Approaches and The Comilla Model,* Publisher: Bangladesh Academy for Rural Development, Kotbari, Comilla, p. 219.

3 *Personal Reminiscences of Change* by Akhter Hameed Khan, Publisher United Nations Children's Fund (UNICEF), March 1994, p. 2.

4 *The Works of Akhter Hameed Khan, Vol II Rural Development Approaches and The Comilla Model,* Publisher:

Bangladesh Academy for Rural Development, Kotbari, Comilla, p. 219.

5 *Personal Reminiscences of Change* by Akhter Hameed Khan, Publisher United Nations Children's Fund (UNICEF), March 1994, p. 1.

6 *Comilla Co-operative Pilot Project (1961-1965)* by A.Aziz Khan, Published by Akhter Hameed Khan, S. Pk., Director, Pakistan Academy for Rural Development, Comilla, East Pakistan, 1965, p. 1.

7 *Rural Development in Action: The Comprehensive Experiment at Comilla, East Pakistan* by Arthur F. Raper, Published by Cornell University Press, Ithaca, NY, USA, p. 47.

8 *Rural Development in Action: The Comprehensive Experiment at Comilla, East Pakistan* by Arthur F. Raper, Published by Cornell University Press, Ithaca, NY, USA, p. 50.

9 *Rural Development in Action: The Comprehensive Experiment at Comilla, East Pakistan* by Arthur F. Raper, Published by Cornell University Press, Ithaca, NY, USA, p. 69.

10 *Rural Development in Action: The Comprehensive Experiment at Comilla, East Pakistan* by Arthur F. Raper, Published by Cornell University Press, Ithaca, NY, USA, p. 59.

11 *Personal Reminiscences of Change* by Akhter Hameed Khan, Publisher United Nations Children's Fund (UNICEF), March 1994, p. 2.

12 *Comilla Co-operative Pilot Project (1961-1965)* by A.Aziz Khan, Published by Akhter Hameed Khan, S. Pk., Director, Pakistan Academy for Rural Development, Comilla, East Pakistan, 1965, p. 4.

13 *Comilla Co-operative Pilot Project (1961-1965)* by A.Aziz Khan, Published by Akhter Hameed Khan, S. Pk., Director, Pakistan Academy for Rural Development, Comilla, East

Pakistan, 1965, p. 4.

14 *Comilla Approach To Rural Development* by Qazi Azher Ali, Published by Director, Pakistan Academy For Rural Development, Comilla, 1966, p. 9.

15 *The Works of Akhter Hameed Khan, Vol. III Rural Works And The Comilla Cooperative*, Published by Bangladesh Academy for Rural Development, Kotbari, Comilla, Bangladesh, p. 144.

16 *Rural Development in Action: The Comprehensive Experiment at Comilla, East Pakistan* by Arthur F. Raper, Published by Cornell University Press, Ithaca, NY, USA, p. 76.

17 An added benefit of the Comilla Cooperatives was that it encouraged and empowered women to become productive participants in the economy.

18 *Comilla Co-operative Pilot Project (1961-1965)* by A.Aziz Khan, Published by Akhter Hameed Khan, S. Pk., Director, Pakistan Academy for Rural Development, Comilla, East Pakistan, 1965, p. 3.

19 *The Works of Akhter Hameed Khan, Vol. III Rural Works And The Comilla Cooperative*, Published by Bangladesh Academy for Rural Development, Kotbari, Comilla, Bangladesh, p. 143.

20 *Comilla Co-operative Pilot Project (1961-1965)* by A.Aziz Khan, Published by Akhter Hameed Khan, S. Pk., Director, Pakistan Academy for Rural Development, Comilla, East Pakistan, 1965, p. 9.

21 *Rural Development in Action: The Comprehensive Experiment at Comilla, East Pakistan* by Arthur F. Raper, Published by Cornell University Press, Ithaca, NY, USA, p. 64.

22 *Rural Development in Action: The Comprehensive Experiment at Comilla, East Pakistan* by Arthur F. Raper,

Published by Cornell University Press, Ithaca, NY, USA, p.p. 64-65.

23 http://www.irm.edu.pk/Movies/Mushraaf.wmv

24 http://www.akrsplessons.org/speeches.php?goto=shaukat

25 *The Life and Times of Dr. Akhter Hameed Khan*, Symposium Report, March 4-5, 2000, Journalism Resource Centre Publications, Islamabad, Pakistan.

26 http://www.irm.edu.pk/ahkrc/ahk_archives.htm

27 Book Reviews by W. Klatt, *Pacific Affairs*, Vol. 44, No.1. (Spring, 1971), Published by University of British Columbia, p.p. 137-138.

28 *Rural Development in Action: The Comprehensive Experiment at Comilla, East Pakistan* by Arthur F. Raper. Published by Cornell University Press, Ithaca, NY, USA, p. vii.

29 *An Organizational Analysis of Rural Development Projects at Comilla, East Pakistan* by Harvey M. Choldin (Michigan State University). *Economic Development and Cultural Change*, Vol. 20, No. 4. (Jul., 1972). Published by University of Chicago Press, p.p. 688-689.

30 *The Development Project as Natural Experiment: The Comilla, Pakistan Projects* by Harvey M. Choldin (Michigan State University). *Economic Development and Cultural Change*, Vol. 17, No. 4. (Jul., 1969). Published by University of Chicago Press, p. 483.

31 *The Green Revolution and "Economic Man": Some Lessons for Community Development in South Asia?* by Harry W. Blair. *Pacific Affairs*, Vol. 44, No. 3 (Autumn, 1971). Published by University of British Columbia, p.p. 361-362.

32 http://www.syberwurx.com/jrc/dialogues/October5.html

33 *Allama Mashriqi & Dr. Akhtar Hameed Khan: Two Legends of Pakistan* by Nasim Yousaf, New York, USA, 2003, p. 409.

34 http://www.irm.edu.pk/Lecture_Rehman_Sobhan.asp

35 *Allama Mashriqi & Dr. Akhtar Hameed Khan: Two Legends of Pakistan* by Nasim Yousaf, New York, USA, 2003, p. 414.

Tribute to Dr Akhter Hameed Khan by Nasim Yousaf

MICRO credit provides very small loans to those who have no verifiable credit history or collateral that would be acceptable to a financial institution. Prior to the micro credit methodology, banks served only the privileged and, as a result, perpetuated the gap between the rich and the poor. However, in the 1950s and 1960s, Dr Akhter Hameed Khan, a world renowned social scientist from Pakistan, initiated the Comilla Cooperative Programme and proved to the world that it was indeed possible to provide credit to the poor.

In order to gain greater understanding of why Dr Khan's cooperative scheme was so successful, one needs to travel back to the 1950s. Since its founding in 1947, the country had been plagued by a number of problems, primarily related to administration and infrastructure, lack of industrialisation, poor communication, a large population, unemployment, and poverty. Problems in the agriculture sector were particularly severe. They included disorganised farming, poor yield, crop damages from floods and pests, lack of application of modern techniques, and improper marketing. Small farmers' landholdings in the villages (in East Pakistan) ranged from one to five acres and they were in a miserable condition.

According to Dr Khan,"90 percent of them owned less than five acres." How had these conditions come about? Therein lies perhaps the greatest challenge of all faced by the small farmers – lack of access to a credit facility. The poor farmers in Pakistan had no creditworthy history or collateral that would be acceptable to the banks and other financial institutions. This meant that the farmers were at the mercy of private lenders, traders, etc. The lenders leveraged their advantageous position to charge high interest rates and earn profits at the expense of the poor. According to Dr Khan, "They (farmers) were short of capital and in their distress borrowed from exorbitant moneylenders and sold to oppressive traders. Small scale agriculture, starved of the capital and skill, damaged by risks, and squeezed by high interest rates and low prices for their output, was in fact going bankrupt." Under such conditions, the impoverished were left with no incentive to learn and adopt modern techniques or increase their per acre agricultural yield.

In an attempt to address these problems, the Government of Pakistan established the Pakistan Academy of Rural Development (PARD). In 1958, Dr Khan was appointed as Director of the newly-formed organisation. The Academy began functioning in May 1959. Dr Khan travelled from village to village to conduct research, gain a more intimate knowledge of the farmers' troubles, and discuss their issues. His focus was on listening rather than dictating.

Speaking with the villagers, Dr Khan quickly recognised that ensuring collaboration between the farmers would be the key to relieving many of their ailments. He came to the conclusion that a cooperative system would be the best means to enable this collaboration. Such a system would allow the farmers to share information, make joint production decisions, and leverage their collective resources to establish a basis for credit-worthiness. Dr Khan emphasised the broad principles of "savings, educational meetings, joint planning and action".

As a result of Dr Khan's efforts, the villagers began to organise and the cooperative experiment at Comilla went underway. By May 1960, ten local cooperatives had been organised. According to author Arthur F. Raper in his book, *Rural Development in Action: The Comprehensive Experiment at Comilla, East Pakistan*, these ten cooperatives comprised "seven village-based agricultural societies, a vegetable growers' society, a women's cooperative, and a weavers' cooperative." Raper further states that by 1961,"Seventeen village societies had…secured 25 loans totalling Rs 108,000. The largest amount borrowed by any village society (cooperative) was Rs 15,000 and the smallest Rs 2,500.These loans were arranged through either the Comilla Cooperative Bank or the Agricultural Bank at Comilla."

As the Comilla experiment matured, there was recognition that a central association was needed to support the local cooperatives (also known as primary cooperatives). So in January 1962, the Kotwali Thana Central Cooperative Association (KTCCA) was registered with Dr Khan as Chairman of its managing committee. Thus, a two-tier system comprised of the cooperatives of small farmers at the local village level and a centralised supporting association at the *thana* level emerged.

The primary cooperative consisted of a group of farmers from a given village (or sometimes multiple villages). In order to participate in the Academy's cooperative programme, they had to meet certain requirements. The KTCCA derived its funds from private as well as public sources, including the government, the Ford Foundation, and the primary cooperatives. Using these funds, it was able to offer loans to the primary cooperatives which, in turn, provided credit to their members. In essence, the Comilla Cooperative had established its own banking system, which for the first time allowed small farmers to obtain loans at low interest rates. Furthermore, it enabled farmers to learn and adopt modern techniques.

Indeed, the Comilla Cooperative started by Dr Khan was no less than a revolution. Perhaps Dr Khan himself best summarized the reasons behind the success of the Comilla programme," The Comilla project proposed a way out of the dilemma of the small village cooperative being economically weak, and the multi-village cooperative lacking in social and psychological cohesion, by establishing a large number of primary groups based on single villages, and federating them into a powerful central association."

In the years subsequent to the founding of the Comilla Cooperative, a number of other initiatives were launched to replicate the success seen at Comilla. Non-agricultural societies modelled after the Comilla Cooperatives were formed in East Pakistan (now Bangladesh) and operated under the Special Cooperative Societies Federation (SCSF).These societies represented such diverse occupations as rickshaw pullers, merchants, butchers, etc. By the middle of 1968, there were

261 agricultural societies and 78 societies in the SCSF.

Meanwhile, in Bangladesh, Professor Muhammad Yunus was closely observing the success of micro credit at the Comilla cooperatives, and in 1983 started the Grameen Bank. He won the 2006 Nobel Peace Prize for his application of micro credit there. In 1989, the Orangi Pilot Project-Orangi Charitable Trust (OPP-OCT) was established in Karachi by Dr Khan as an independent institution to provide micro credit in the urban and the rural areas. In August 2000, Khushali Bank was formed in Pakistan to provide micro credit. Today, the concept of micro credit is being applied in many countries around the world, thanks in large part to Dr Khan's efforts at Comilla.

Dr Khan has proven to the world that the poor can be effective participants in the economy if given the opportunity. Dr Khan's contributions to rural development, poverty alleviation, and the micro credit scheme will surely live on forever. Professor Muhammad Yunus, 2006 Nobel Peace Prize winner and admirer of Dr Khan (in his letter sent on the occasion of a symposium on the 'Life and Times of Dr Khan', held in Islamabad from March 02-05, 2000) wrote, "He (Dr Khan) was so much ahead of everybody else that he was seen more as a 'misfit' than appreciated for his greatness. Dr Khan needs to be rediscovered in the light of the realities and needs of the emerging century." Dr Ishrat Hussain (while he was at the World Bank) said,"…Today micro credit has become a buzzword in the lexicon of development practitioners for poverty alleviation throughout the world, but 35 years ago this idea was pioneered in Comilla."

Dr Akhter Hameed Khan's eighth death anniversary was celebrated yesterday, October 9, 2007

7th Death Anniversary – A Tribute to Dr. Akhter Hameed Khan by Nasim Yousaf

October 9th marked the death anniversary of Dr. Akhter Hameed Khan. He left us seven years ago but his teachings and concepts have continued to revolutionize the world. Professor Muhammad Yunus' winning of the 2006 Nobel Peace Prize is not only an honorable achievement for him but it is also a tribute to Dr. Akhter Hameed Khan, as Khan sahib laid the foundation of microcredit (microfinance) in Comilla academy in Bangladesh.

It is of great importance for us to remember and learn from Dr. Akhter Hameed Khan, who was the originator of the idea of microcredit and of many key advancements in development and poverty alleviation.

*****

A rare giant among men, Dr. Khan pioneered the microcredit concept that would change the finance arena, and he did so in an inconspicuous and uncelebrated manner! Prior to his microcredit scheme, banks were highly reluctant to sanction loans to the poor without any collateral. Their doors were closed to billions of people around the world, because these poor souls did not have a verifiable credit history, had nothing to offer to secure a loan and were essentially seen as a credit-risky population. NOBODY realized that among these poor people were those who were highly talented, honest and hard working. If given the opportunity, they could lift themselves out of poverty and become productive contributors of the economic and financial sectors. However, the banks served only the already privileged and perpetuated the gap between the poor and rich. The poor had no choice but to depend on charity or private lenders, who took all of the profits, leaving the poor poor.

A new solution was desperately needed. Dr. Khan introduced the revolutionary idea of microcredit, thereby opening a new door for billions of destitute and underprivileged. As head of the Pakistan Academy for Rural Development (now Bangladesh Academy for Rural Development, BARD) in Comilla, Bangladesh, Dr. Akhter Hameed Khan pioneered microcredit through a farmers/village cooperatives program. Hence, the first microcredit poverty alleviation project was started at this academy.

Dhiraj Kumar Nath, Secretary, Rural Development and Co-operatives Division, presented a paper in the International Seminar held on 8th - 9th January 2003 in Dhaka, Bangladesh on "Attacking Poverty with Microcredit." He wrote:

"'Comilla Model' developed by the Bangladesh [then East Pakistan] Academy for Rural Development (BARD) in 1960. This model was also largely based on a group approach and providing micro-credit to the co-operators."

Khan Ferdousour Rahman wrote in The Financial Express of Dacca, Bangladesh on August 10, 2006, under the title "Micro-credit operation: Should the MFIs pay tax or not?":

"Perhaps, no other development tool has attracted so much global attention in the history of poverty-focused development efforts than micro-credit... Mr. Akhter Hamid Khan of Bangladesh Academy for Rural Development (BARD) started it in Comilla in the then East Pakistan."

I remember a visit to Dr. Khan's house in Comilla in 1969. While in Comilla, I had firsthand experience of the tremendous respect and love that Dr. Khan and his family received from everyone. This was apparent from the people I met and all the photos of Dr. Khan that I saw in various shops, houses and other places.

Few months prior to the fall of Dacca, Dr. Khan, who loved the people of Bangladesh, very reluctantly moved to Pakistan. But in Pakistan too, people loved Dr. Khan. In 1980, he founded the Orangi Pilot Project (OPP), a poverty alleviation project, in

Karachi, Pakistan. OPP also introduced the microcredit scheme in the 1980s.

Meanwhile, the Grameen Bank was born in 1983 in Bangladesh and was based on the concept of microcredit / microfinance initiated in Dr. Khan's rural academy at Comilla. Professor Yunus institutionalized Dr. Khan's microcredit scheme through the Grameen Bank and made history in the arena of poverty alleviation. Indeed! Professor Yunus deserves heartiest congratulations for his unparalleled accomplishment.

Professor Muhammad Yunus, you may call him a disciple or an admirer of Dr. Khan, sent a letter on the occasion of a symposium held in Islamabad on the Life and Times of Dr. Khan (March 02-05, 2000) and praised Dr. Khan:

"He was one of the greatest human beings of the past century... Dr. Khan needs to be rediscovered... We have a lot to discover and a whole lot to learn from him."

In Pakistan, following Dr. Khan's proven experiments, the Khushali Bank was set up in August 2000. This was the first major initiative to bridge the demand for microfinance services.

The then Governor of State Bank of Pakistan, Dr. Ishrat Hussain, privileged me with his comments on Dr. Khan, in his letter dated September 10, 2001. He wrote:

"The recent initiatives taken by us in establishing Khushali Bank and the Microfinance institutions in the private sector are a testimony to the robustness of the approach adopted by him [Dr. Khan] and the leadership provided by Doctor Sahib in this field."

In his address at the Dr. Akhter Hameed Khan Memorial Lecture in Islamabad (May 23, 2002), the President of Khushali Bank, Ghalib Nishtar, appreciated Dr. Khan and his concept. He stated:

" …in the context of poverty alleviation and Micro-finance, we all know the Comilla and the Orangi Pilot Projects, which are the very role models for development institutions around the world…"

*****

Indeed, Dr. Khan's ideas have revolutionized banking and economic / human development and are playing a pivotal role in poverty alleviation around the world. Dr. Khan's concepts and ideas proved to the world that the poor were creditworthy, and that if given the opportunity, their energies could contribute positively to economic activity. This stunned the gurus of the finance world, and today, this concept has been replicated in many countries around the globe. Microcredit terminology did not even exist in the finance arena, until the idea was initiated by Dr. Khan.

In the words of Dr. Ishrat Hussain, when he was at the World Bank:

"…Today micro-credit has become a buzzword in the lexicon of development practitioners for poverty alleviation throughout the world but 35 years ago this idea was pioneered in Comilla."

Microcredit and microfinance have expanded and grown tremendously since the origination of the idea by Dr. Khan. As a result of Dr. Khan's original efforts and the efforts that followed from other development experts, such as Professor Yunus, microfinance exploded on the global scene. Today, with the microcredit / microfinance system in place in many countries, access to loans and other financial services, regardless of gender and economic status, have paved the way for poor to earn their livelihood with respect and dignity. This has brought self esteem to the poor and has substantially contributed to removing socio-economic imbalances and promoting economic development around the globe.

Today, BARD, established in 1959 by Khan sahib, continues to play an important role, and the academy is known, at home and abroad, for its evolved model "Comilla Approach to Rural Development." BARD was given the National Award in 1986 for its outstanding performance and contribution in rural development.

Dr. Khan's Orangi Pilot Project also continues to make significant contributions to development. Besides implementing its own projects, it also serves as a training institution. A large number of non-governmental organizations, non-profit organizations, advisors, consultants, students, and the like, from Pakistan and abroad, visit and learn from OPP's experiences. For example, the National Commission for Human Development, which started in Pakistan in 2002, operates on similar concepts and conducts similar projects in the social sector, as what Dr. Khan had applied in the OPP.

In addition to creating institutions, Dr. Khan also trained countless number of people, including officers of the Civil Service of Pakistan (CSP). Ex-President of Pakistan, Sardar Farooq Ahmad Khan Leghari and Ex-Governor State Bank, Dr. Ishrat Hussain, are among his pupils, who took the training at Comilla as CSP officers.

Dr. Khan was a mentor for renowned personalities of Pakistan and Bangladesh. Those who learned from Dr. Khan have made great contribution towards human development within their respective areas of expertise in Pakistan and Bangladesh. Their contributions are being well-acclaimed. Besides the respected and great humanist, Professor Muhammad Yunus, at least four others have earned the Ramon Magsaysay Award from the Philippines. Those great men are:

-Shoaib Sultan Khan in 1992 (Pakistan)

-Tasneem Ahmed Siddiqui in 1999 (Pakistan)

-Tahrunnesa Ahmed Abdullah in 1978 (Bangladesh)

-Mohammad Yeasin in 1988 (Bangladesh)

Indisputably! Khan sahib was a pioneer of development methodology in the true sense. His innovative approach to non-governmental / non-profit organizations shaped human development around the world.

*****

Dr. Akhter Hameed Khan left us on October 09, 1999. On his death, media and many distinguished personalities and organizations from around the globe, paid rich tributes to this great soul of the 20th century. From among those who always admire him, I cannot exclude Shoaib Sultan Khan, who requires no introduction. Shoaib Sultan Khan, a distinguished and well acclaimed personality of Pakistan, paid his tribute to Khan sahib, which I had the privilege of quoting in a biography of Allama Mashriqi and Dr. Akhter Hameed Khan that I wrote a few years ago. Shoaib Sultan Khan stated:

"In all my travels throughout the world, I have never come across a person of the stature of Akhtar Hameed Khan. I sometimes wonder did Pakistan really make the best use of his unique experience with which he was so willing and keen to benefit his countrymen and women. But now it is too late even to ask this question. The country has missed an opportunity of a century."

On Dr. Khan's death, the World Bank wrote:

"While his long and distinguished career in social service is replete with success stories, the Orangi Pilot Project deserves special mention for providing, among other things, a sewerage system to one of the largest settlements in Asia on a self-help basis, and introducing micro-credits to disadvantaged individuals to help them earn a respectable livelihood."

With Khan sahib's death, poor people around the globe felt orphaned. But Dr. Khan left behind his methodology and techniques, from which billions of deprived people continue to benefit and will continue to do so for a long time to come.

Hameedah Begum – The Woman Behind the Great Dr. A.H. Khan by Nasim Yousaf

A Tribute on Her 90th Birth Anniversary

Behind Every Great Man, There is a Great Woman

Hameedah Begum was born to a pre-eminent political leader of South Asia, Allama Mashraqi, and later became wife of globally acclaimed Dr. Akhtar Hameed Khan. She was the eldest daughter of Mashraqi and his first wife (Walayat Begum). She was unpretentious, strong, and selfless, as is evident by her way of life.

Hameedah Begum was born in Peshawar on December 25, 1920. She was good in her studies and like her father, she was very good in Mathematics and completed her education with distinction. This was a great achievement at the time, when women were hardly encouraged to acquire an education.

I learned many things about Hameedah Begum (my aunt) from my beloved mother (Masuda Yousaf). According to my mother, Hameedah Begum (along with her family) took keen interest in her father's political life and participated in her father's Khaksar Movement's activities. She being the eldest was among the top confidants of Mashraqi. During the freedom struggle, when the family's activities and home were under constant surveillance by plain clothed detectives of C.I.D. and Mashraqi was imprisoned, Hameedah Begum maintained her demeanor and kept up the morale of her younger siblings. My mother used to tell us stories of this time; speaking of police raids, she said, "most police raids were held at night when the family would be fast asleep. The armed men would surround the house and would take positions on the roof and walls. The sounds of heavy boots would generally wake us up. Police breaking into the house in the darkness used to be very scary but none of us were intimidated by police actions." Furthermore, "Your grandfather used to be under close watch all the time by intelligence agencies and threat messages were a regular feature, but we never bothered about them." In the face of such difficult and tense times, Hameedah Begum as the eldest child stood firm and never lost her courage.

Towards the end of 1939 (after Mashraqi's release from Lucknow jail), *Nikkah* between Hameedah Begum and Dr. Akhtar Hameed Khan was solemnized in Icchra. However, *Rukhsati* (departure from her parents' house) was to take place at a later date. Unfortunately, the *Rukhsati* was delayed as, in March 1940, Mashraqi was imprisoned. Hameedah Begum was highly saddened that the Government refused to release her father, even for a few hours, to attend her marriage and send the newly married couple off with his blessings. In addition, a dowry could not be given at the time as the Government refused to release Mashraqi's bank account to draw money for it. This however was not a concern for Hameedah Begum and later, when a dowry was presented to them, Hameedah Begum and Dr. Khan donated it.

In 1943, Hameedah Begum was distressed by the Bengal Famine, which took an estimated three million lives (death toll higher than the two World Wars); she and her husband were disappointed by the overall handling of the situation by the Government to help the suffering masses. With his wife's support, Dr. Khan decided to resign and become a laborer, in order to find solutions to poverty by embracing the lifestyle of the poor. This was a turning point in their lives. All of a sudden, Hameedah Begum went from being the wife of a powerful ICS officer to a completely different lifestyle. People resorted to backbiting, but Hameedah Begum paid no attention to this and stood behind Dr. Khan's decision.

Soon the couple's house became a laboratory to find solutions to change the destiny of their fellow countrymen. Alongside her husband, Hameedah Begum got a chance to see poverty closely, but she never complained of the hard times they went through and never pushed Dr. Khan to quit the experiment and get a job, which would have been easy for him given his credentials. The experiment continued until 1947, when Dr. Zakir Hussain (who later became President of India) then head of Jamia Millia Islamia (Delhi) persuaded Dr. Khan to join his educational institution.

While the couple was in Delhi, Ch. Muhammad Ali (who later became Prime Minister of Pakistan) asked Dr. Khan to move to Karachi. In 1950, the couple moved to Karachi and in the same year to Comilla. Upon arrival, Hameedah Begum witnessed poverty stricken Bengalis and refugees. Dr. Khan engaged himself in changing the lives of people and later succeeded in founding the renowned Bangladesh (previously Pakistan) Academy for Rural Development. Dr. Khan's hard work received world acclamation and he could not have attained this success without his wife. She had sacrificed herself alongside him, did not demand his time, and in his absence, took care of their children; importantly she gave him the peace of mind Dr. Khan needed to meet his dream.

In addition to supporting her husband's mission, many are unaware of the fact that Hameedah Begum provided working capital and set up a factory (cottage industry) in the compound of her house, so that the local poor could earn and live comfortably. The factory was named, *Mrs. Khan Printing & Weaving Factory*. Here, about twenty Bengalis and *Muhajirs* (refugees) produced silk *Banarsi* and cotton *Sarees* (wraparounds) and cotton *Chaddars* (shawls); cotton *Sarees* and *Chaddars* were then block-printed. In addition, Hameedah Begum sacrificed a room of her house for an artist who needed small working capital and a place to work; he handcrafted and painted Asian wooden figurines. All the products produced in these units were sold in the market and the income was distributed among the workers; no income was retained by Hameedah Begum. She and Dr. Khan would sometimes laugh that her factory generated more income to feed twenty families than what Dr. Khan was drawing as a salary.

Throughout, Hameedah Begum led an unadorned life. According to her daughter, Amina Khan "she would not wear jewelry or fashionable outfits. She was not picky and ate all kinds of food; she loved desserts and drinking *lassi* and *skanjbeen.*" Even though her husband was entitled to a higher salary, luxury house, and fancy car as the top man of the Academy, neither he took this benefit nor did she push him to. She was content with what they had. Further, she never sought glorification, e.g. when President Ayub Khan offered Dr. Khan the positions of Governorship, Vice Chancellor of Dhaka University, or Advisor to the President. And she never used Mashraqi or her husband's name to seek the limelight. This was a woman who was born with a silver spoon in her mouth and in her childhood had been looked after by a Nanny and British governess (at the time, Mashraqi led a high profile life); yet she preferred and led an unassuming life. She was down to earth and above worldly possessions.

At a time when unfortunately women did not have as much public power, Hameedah Begum stood strong behind her father and husband to support the elevation of her fellow countrymen. She actively participated in her father's movement to bring freedom to the country. With her husband, she committed to leading a selfless life and demonstrated, through her own projects as well as support of her husband's work, her commitment to helping the poor. Dr. Khan could not have accomplished his goals and earned many awards including nomination for the Nobel Peace Prize, if Hameedah Begum had resisted Dr. Khan's resignation as an ICS officer and forced him to lead a conventional life. Throughout all this, she also dedicated herself to her children. In Amina Khan's words, "My mother was a great human being and she always cared for the people. Though she lived a short life, she was an accomplished woman."

On May 16, 1966, while on a trip to the then West Pakistan, Hameedah Begum died at her father's house in Ichhra

(Lahore). She was suffering from acute diabetes. She was buried at Miani Sahib grave yard. On her death, Dr. Khan dedicated a poem, *Hameedah Begum.*

Though Hameedah Begum passed away, she left behind an exemplary model for women, particularly in developing nations, to follow. Mothers in these nations need to guide their children, as Hameedah Begum stood behind her husband, to seek *real success* – success that is not defined by short term goals of owning a fancy car and/or possessing a luxury house but real success that strives to make innovative contributions toward the good of humankind. Mothers need to encourage their children to bring forward ground-breaking discoveries/inventions and act selflessly, as such contributions can only revolutionize Pakistan and its poor image for the better.

Dr. Akhter Hameed Khan: An Appreciation by Norman Uphoff, Cornell University

Akhter Hameed Khan was always a teacher, but in his own style, not the aloof *guru* of Sanskritic creed. He exhibited the introspective but active propensities of an Arjuna, a warrior and a battler who was nonetheless gentle and reflective, not seeking conflict but not shrinking from it either when there were people and principles to be served. Whether making waves in the Indian civil service before subcontinental independence, or insisting on high standards as a school principal, or encouraging small farmers around Comilla in East Pakistan (later Bangladesh) to form cooperatives, or working with Pathan tribesmen in the North West Frontier Province of Pakistan, or walking the crowded periurban lanes of Orangi, he was always engaging others to think about their condition and their possibilities in new and self-critical ways. I do not know what his life was like when he assigned himself to live and work in a village as a locksmith in Aligarh, India, after leaving the ICS, but he probably spent more time explaining to clients what needed to be done to their errant locks than he did on the actual repairs.

I was unfortunate never to have known Akhter Hameed intimately— knowing him mostly through several close friends and then having several memorable occasions together—yet I nevertheless considered him one of my gurus for rural development, having much wisdom to impart and teaching by his example as much as by his words. One of my closest friends from graduate school days at Princeton, Blake Hendee Smith, now himself passed on, had the great good fortune of getting a first job at the Academy for Rural Development in Comilla after completing his MPA at the Woodrow Wilson School. Blake's letters to me were so full of admiring comments about the works and words of Akhter Hameed that I came to feel as though I had an acquaintance with the man himself within just one year.

Subsequently, I got to know well Edgar (Ted) Owens with the

U.S. Agency for International Development's Asia Bureau, and then its Office of Rural Development, who was an unabashed admirer of Akhter Hameed from having become acquainted at Comilla. Ted, who has also passed on, was someone who had few heroes because of his very sharp eyes for detecting feet of clay. But he had only praise for Akhter Hameed, whom he considered his guru for rural development. When Ted wrote *Development Reconsidered* (Lexington Books, 1972) with Robert de A. Shaw, the influence of Akhter Hameed's thinking and experience was evident throughout the book, as much of the impetus for Ted's original rethinking of development strategy had come from discussions and observations at the Comilla academy.

During that time, I was serving as chair of the Rural Development Committee at Cornell University, an interdisciplinary group supported by Cornell University's Center for International Studies. With prompting from Ted Owens and funding that he mobilized from USAID, we began working on issues and experiences of participatory rural development. The summary monograph that I wrote with Milton Esman in 1974—based on 18 case studies of rural development experience ranging from China, Korea and Japan in East Asia to Egypt, Turkey and Yugoslavia on the edges of West Asia (*Local Organization for Rural Development: Analysis of Asian Experience*, Rural Development Committee, Cornell University)— was very much influenced by the Comilla case. This was documented and analyzed by our colleague Harry Blair in his monograph *The Elusiveness of Equity: Institutional Approaches to Rural Development in Bangladesh* (Rural Development Committee, Cornell University, 1974). When Macmillan Publishers subsequently decided to publish the case studies and analyses in a three-volume book, *Rural Development and Local Organization in Asia* (New Delhi, 1982-83), it was most appropriate that I dedicate this large compendium mapping out the terrain of participatory rural development across Asia to Akhter Hameed Khan along with Ted Owens.

In 1977, the Rural Development Committee was pleased to

have Akhter Hameed visit Cornell as one of the resource persons for a workshop on rural development that we had organized for staff of the United Nations. One of the most memorable evenings of my life was spent with Akhter Hameed discussing the impending parliamentary elections in India, which Indira Gandhi had called to ratify her autocratic rule, imposed through her declaration of a state of emergency in 1975. Akhter Hameed and I were surprised and pleased to find someone else—each other—who believed that Indian voters were going to defy Mrs. Gandhi's plans and turn her government out of office.

This was a prediction that few observers were prepared to make at the time, but we both had concluded that there would be an upset. Since I am trained as a political scientist, I am supposed to be able to discern such things, but in Akhter Hameed's case, he drew on no academic training. He had a deep knowledge of rank-and-file Indians, along with other South Asians whom he knew in Pakistan and Bangladesh, and an equally deep confidence in their willingness to stand up to tyranny, even the home-grown variety. The Indian electorate acted with courage and consistency to take their democracy back from Indira's autocratic hands.

Thereafter, I followed from afar Akhter Hameed's contributions to rural development in the North West Frontier Province, appreciating his reports on participatory irrigation management there as my own rural development work had drawn me into this subject in Sri Lanka (*Learning from Gal Oya: Possibilities for Participatory Development and Post-Newtonian Social Science*, Cornell University Press, 1992; republished by Intermediate Technology Publications, 1996). Akhter Hameed was also one of the originators of the Aga Khan Rural Support Programme in the northern districts of Pakistan, now one of the best known initiatives to promote rural development under remote and difficult physical and sociological conditions. I don't know the circumstances for his moving southward in 1980 to take up an even greater challenge, in a squatter colony known as Orangi housing almost 1 million persons outside of Karachi. But this in my view turned out to be—starting at age 65, when most other mortals are moving into retirement—the most inspiring and single-handed accomplishment of his career.

Akhter Hameed would be the first to object to my calling this a "single-handed accomplishment," since indeed, it was a collective achievement involving hundreds of persons in leadership roles, and many thousands more in important supporting roles. But this was a creation of a single, marvelous mind, one with great experience and confidence in participatory development. His idea mobilized the talents and imagination of tens of thousands of persons commonly characterized as "common." They embellished and extended the idea, being persons actually endowed with capacities beyond most others' imagination, and maybe initially even beyond their own expectations.

It was the genius of Akhter Hameed that he could see this potential and knew how to evoke it. His story of how the Orangi Pilot Project got its start, how it made its way through the initial years, how it expanded its scope and deepened its roots, is told in a chapter that he contributed to a book that I edited with my colleagues Anirudh Krishna and Milton J. Esman, *Reasons for Hope: Instructive Experiences in Rural Development* (Kumarian Press, 1997; Vistaar Publications, New Delhi, 1998). We stretched the definition of "rural" to include his memoire in this volume, because the Orangi Pilot Project was one of the best applications of the *principles and philosophy* of participatory rural development that we could find anywhere in the world. One of the simplest and most impressive statistics, apart from the nearly 1 million persons who eventually benefited from this initiative, is the fact that for every rupee of external funding that was received for this work, *17 rupees* worth of labor, materials and management were contributed by the communities participating in this effort. This is one of the best examples of self-reliant and sustainable development in practice, an approach more often advocated than realized.

Having accomplished many important things in three major

countries during his lifetime, Akhter Hameed remained modest and eager to learn into his 80s. In 1997 I sent him the manuscript for a companion volume that Esman, Krishna and I had written, *Reasons for Success: Learning from Instructive Experiences in Rural Development* (Kumarian Press and Vistaar Publications, 1998), inviting his suggestions and criticisms to strengthen it before its publication. He sent back a number of helpful comments, but said that he wanted to keep the manuscript because he had found it useful "as an instructional manual and reference book" and wanted to share it with others. For me, there could have been no greater praise from a person whom I had always admired and from whom I had learned so much over three decades. But Akhter Hameed was an unusual guru, always looking for ways to advance his understanding of the human condition and to improve the situation of others.

The book *Reasons for Success* reflects many of the lessons that we and others have learned from Akhter Hameed's long and pioneering lifetime of creative work on behalf of the poor and disadvantaged. He did not see the poor as lacking in intelligence and character—only as lacking in the material and organizational means to become more productive, for themselves and for their families and their society. He took it upon himself to try to get for them reliable access to credit, functioning cooperatives, relevant training, and cultural values that would strengthen their capacities and determination to put poverty behind themselves and to become more autonomous and free-spirited. He wanted to see and hear common people act and speak with uncommon determination and boldness. This to him was the essence of development—changing inherited circumstances, keeping practices and ideas that had meaning and value to people, while engaging in new ones that could promote human values more effectively.

Sadly, such towering figures and lofty intellects as Akhter Hameed's are quite uncommon. Only a few emerge in any generation. His lifetime spanned an era of incredible change, with remarkable advances in certain political and economic respects, and lamentable failings in these same realms. What is clear is that South Asia would be a poorer and a less noble part of the world today without his life-long efforts on behalf of his fellow men and women. It is left to those who follow him and learned from him to continue these efforts.

Reflections on the Distinguished Career of Dr. Akhter Hameed Khan by George H. Axinn, Michigan State University

In my mind and heart, the greatest professional and human contribution to rural development in the second half of the 20th Century was made by Akhter Hameed Khan. He was a man of great stature, and also a humble man. He tested the best globally recognized ideas of scholars and practitioners of rural development—and explained their strengths and their weaknesses to those who were seriously interested. He added a depth of understanding beyond anything the world had previously recognized. Akhter Hameed shared the depth of his continuing learning in the most human, sensitive, warm, and yet challenging manner. He enhanced both his written and spoken words with simple examples drawn from the lives of the rural people to whom he dedicated his life. And he did that with a rhetorical elegance which set him apart, and far above, the other practitioners and scholars of his generation.

In Manila, Philippines, the Ramon Magsaysay Award Foundation selected Dr. Khan as the 1963 Awardee for Government Service. At the conclusion of their citation, they stated, "In electing Akhtar Hameed Khan to receive the 1963 Ramon Magsaysay Award for Government Service, the Board of Trustees recognizes his inspiring personal commitment of experience, erudition, and energy to scientific testing and application of a workable formula for rural emancipation among his people."

At a workshop on "Development from Below" in October, 1973 in Addis Ababa, Ethiopia, Akhter Hameed opened with these words: "I think I was imprudent when I agreed to write this paper. I am a migrant from—not a resident of—Bangladesh. I possess little knowledge of her present affairs. In the past, to my discomfort, I was sometimes called Mr. Comilla. A total disconnection looks like an act of poetic justice by the gods, who have decreed that no more shall the people of Comilla be harassed by my antics, nor I be overwhelmed by their problems. I am now merely the ghost of Comilla. Instead of fading away, it is impertinent on my part to haunt a rural development workshop in Addis Ababa. A ghost does not know the facts of today; he only shuffles the fictions of yesterday. He cannot tell what should be done. At best he can tell what he tried to do. I call myself an expert in failure. If anyone wants to learn from my example, I am glad to be examined. Dissect me as you please."

In that same talk, after one of the most useful and widely applicable statements about *rural development* which has even been made (That is my personal assessment as a fellow scholar/practitioner who has labored in this same vineyard, in Africa, Asia, and the Americas for more than half a century) Akhtar Hameed went on to say:

"At the end I must apologize for the egoism of a personal narrative. I am ashamed that I have come out in the limelight. I sincerely believe that the Academy's work was decidedly a collective effort. There were many partners in this enterprise— the instructors, the foreign advisors and experts, the government officials, the people of Comilla. Their contributions were vital. I was made a figurehead not because I hankered to be one, but because people want figureheads and scapegoats. In some ways I cut a sorry figure. I was not proud and assertive. I was diffident and skeptical. I was not possessive. Repeatedly I sought retirement. At intervals I felt twinges of my old disillusion. Often, after a distracting day, I found peace in Sufi poetry or Buddhist scriptures. I was shaken by Sufi's admonition: 'You tarry and Time runs. You plan and Fate smiles.' And I pondered over the noble Buddhist truths: 'Life is full of sorrow, the cause of sorrow is desire, extinguish desire so that sorrow may cease.' Then I fell asleep and dreamt that I was a kitten trying to catch my tail."

What an eloquent scholar/practitioner from whom to learn! What an inspiring teacher from whom to learn! What a humble genius from whom to discover wisdom! Small wonder that I so quickly agreed to the opportunity to contribute to this book in his memory!

My first meeting with Akhtar Hameed came in 1958, when he came to the campus of Michigan State University. He led a group of newly employed staff of the nascent East Pakistan Academy for Village Development at a place called Comilla, and was accompanied by a similar group from the West Pakistan Academy for Village Development at Peshawar. Michigan State had been working with the Government of Pakistan and with the Ford Foundation in the establishment of these two new institutions. They were established to train staff for the Village Aid Program, that was then doing rural development work in both East and West Pakistan.

At that time, I directed a program at MSU called the Institute for Extension Personnel Development, and provided masters degree programs for practicing extension personnel from various parts of the USA, as well as from other countries. For some reason, the managers of the "Pakistan Program" sent Akhtar Hameed and his colleagues to me for a special course on how to do agricultural extension work.

For some participants, this may have been a useful academic exercise. We did have seminars, and traveled around the state visiting extension activities. But, for Akhtar Hameed, who was far ahead of me in knowledge, experience, and understanding of everything discussed in the course, especially with respect to its application within Pakistan, it should have been an insult. He was, of course, very polite, and a good participant in the group. But he was often absent from the seminars. Later I discovered that he made a habit of going to the library, where he read avidly about topics that were more relevant than anything I had to offer. He studied the Danish Folk Schools movement of years ago. He studied the early cooperatives in England, how they were organized, and how they operated. He would often sit under a tree on the beautiful lawns in the center of the MSU campus, concentrating on his reading of these things, as well as the Koran and other religious/philosophical writings. He was busy learning about relevant matters, many of which he later deployed at Comilla.

In retrospect, I learned much much more from Akhtar Hameed than he learned from me.

My next encounter with Akhter Hameed came in 1963, when I was serving as Coordinator of Michigan State University's Nigeria Program, and traveling constantly between responsibilities at the University of Nigeria in Nsukka and Enugu, and resource bases at the University of London, the US Agency for International Development in Washington, and the campus of Michigan State in East Lansing. Thanks to Dr. Glenn L. Taggart, then Dean of International Programs at MSU, and my mentor, I was diverted to accompany Dean Taggart to visit several other MSU international activities—in West Pakistan, in India, in East Pakistan, in Okinawa, and in Taiwan.

After several days at the West Pakistan Academy for Village Development in Peshawar, and visits with the Ford Foundation leadership in New Delhi, India, Glenn set off to meet MSU personnel working near Madras, and I traveled alone to Comilla. It was a memorable journey, as tensions were high between India and Pakistan, and Indian Airlines had few of its regular aircraft available for such passenger flights. We flew a circuitous route, with several different domestic stops before arriving in Dhaka long after the flight to Comilla had left. Pakistani immigration officers were quite skeptical of me, and questioned me at length on where I was going, and how I expected to get there. My first thought was to stay the night in Dhaka, and take the next available flight, but airport personnel assured me that there was an international conference just begun there, and there were no available hotel rooms in the city. I attempted to phone the Ford Foundation in Dhaka and the Academy for Village Development in Comilla, but could not get through to either. After a while, I set off by taxi to double check the availability of a hotel room, but that effort also failed.

Sharing my frustration, my creative taxi driver came up with a better idea. He suggested the railroad, which had trains to

Chittagong from Dhaka, and those stopped en route in Comilla. That resulted in a lovely first class journey aboard the *Green Arrow*, a train which did take me to Comilla. Unmet there by anyone from the Academy, as none of my several messages had gotten through, and having an excess of luggage and packages for the Academy, I hired two bicycle rickshaws and set off for the wrong place. Without any Bengali language, and having forgotten that I was supposed to go to Rani Kuti (formerly the "queen's cottage") I had another unscheduled scenic tour of beautiful rice paddy country. At one point we moved to the side of the road to let a vehicle hurrying in the opposite direction pass by us. It was loaded with Peace Corps volunteers. By good fortune, they realized that I didn't know where I was going, and convinced my two rickshaw drivers to load all my things into their vehicle, and helped me pay them.

Eventually, I arrived at the project headquarters, which also had lodging and food service for several foreign "advisors." And, to my delight, Akhtar Hameed met me there with plans for a very busy few days. Our travel from then on was by foot, mostly walking rapidly on the narrow bunds between rice paddies. Akhtar Hameed was lecturing as we went along, speaking clearly so I could easily understand him, but walking so fast that I often had to break into a run to catch up. He answered questions, explained the nuances of *why* some things happened as they did, provided insights in depth, and never slowed down his walk. We visited village committees, village leaders, and meetings of village cooperatives.

When Akhtar Hameed and his staff had returned to Comilla from their studies at Michigan State, the staff was eager to start some of the activities they had been exploring. But he would not allow that. Instead, he insisted that they invest at least one full year in learning about the people of Cotowali Thana, the district adjacent to Comilla. Only after that would the new Thana development center be allowed to begin actual projects. So he and his colleagues walked from village to village, from house to house, from field to field. They observed the people's daily lives; they visited with people; they listened to people. They learned, first hand, to see the world as local people saw it!

By the time I first visited, many activities had begun. One principle Akhtar Hameed learned became a guiding strategy for many of us who later followed. As he put it, "Rural development requires a comprehensive and coordinated program involving all government departments operating in that area." Another was that "the civil administration must collaborate with local self-governing units." Decades later, while serving as FAO Representative in India, my colleagues were able to implement that principle in the new "watershed management programs."

Following Ahktar Hameed in my first visit, I observed that sometimes village meetings were after dark, with only one kerosene lantern at the desk, so the chairperson could follow an agenda, or so that the accountant could record payments. Each member's name was called, and the individual walked up and paid some money (often less than a rupee) as weekly dues. That was recorded in the individual's account. The social pressure forced everyone to pay at least something at each meeting. The alternative was to stay home and (pretend to) be ill. Anyone who failed to attend several consecutive weekly meetings was dropped from the cooperative. The discipline, which Akhtar Hameed insisted upon, was a major factor in the success of the savings and investment program.

Many other aspects of the Comilla "experiment" were demonstrated to me personally by Akhtar Hameed during that week. He viewed all these activities as part of the trial and error process by means of which the staff of the Academy would learn how to facilitate rural development more effectively than the world expected. Many times, years later, I heard him tell others that there was no "Comilla approach." There were many different programs and projects; some worked much better than others; and some aspects of what was attempted proved to be quite useful.

Among the aspects he demonstrated to me was the possibility of conducting projects for rural women, even in a society that protected women by keeping them within the home. As in other approaches he and his colleagues attempted, he met with the local religious leaders (Imams). He met them individually and in groups. When they approved a particular activity, Akhtar Hameed and his colleagues tried it. So it was with the programs for rural women. In one successful program for women, the Academy paid for a rickshaw puller to meet the woman at her home, and, with her husband or father accompanying her, took them to the training center. There, groups of women met in a classroom, while their men had tea and conversations nearby. They even dealt with such sensitive issues as family planning.

These and many other "successful" approaches at Comilla have been well documented in the literature. In this paper, I merely give these as examples as illustrations of my personal encounters. Over the years, at Michigan State University, there were many more discussions with Akhtar Hameed.

On one occasion, from 1976 thru 1978, while I was living in a remote rural village in Nepal for two years, Akhter Hameed was a visiting professor at Michigan State. MSU assigned him to my office during my absence. Upon my return, as he was preparing to depart, he presented me with a gift of one of Wendell Berry's most significant books on the changing rural scene in the USA. Through that, Akhtar taught me several additional lessons about rural development. And he joined my wife Nancy and me in several seminars during the period of our overlap on the same campus. Some of those discussions were recorded, and continue to be a source of inspiration.

Another inspiration was Akhtar Hameed's later work in the urban Orangi Pilot Project, a very poor section of the city of Karachi. There he employed the lessons learned in rural places to communities of rural people who had migrated to an urban slum. At one point, in the early 1980's he drove me through the narrow streets of Orangi, driving his own jeep, carefully avoiding many local people walking those streets. It was obvious to me that they all knew him, appreciated his efforts on their behalf, and loved him. He documents that stage of his life in his book, *Orangi Pilot Project—Reminiscences and*

Reflections, published by Oxford University Press in 1996.

For me personally, as for many others whose life-task has been the improvement of the human condition for those who live in rural places, Akhtar Hameed left thousands of inspiring and encouraging words. I close with a few of those from his essay entitled "My Troubled Life" (Presented under the University Extension Lectures series at the University of Peshawar, Pakistan on April 24, 1983, available in *The Collected Works of Akhter Hameed Khan,* Vol. I, pp. vii-xxi). Would that I have the wisdom to realize how well these same words of his fit me now.

"Old men are bores. They are boring because whenever they find a young audience, they pose as preachers and utter virtuous platitudes. They speak of a glorious ancient past and a glorious remote future as if both belonged to them, as if both were their children, as if the poor beggars knew the alchemy of past and future glory. But the young listeners know that the fake vendors of glory have made a dirty mess of our recent past and present." …

"My generation has played its part, and is now departing from the scene. I too am ready for departure. I passed a confused and rambling life in an insecure and turbulent world. Therefore my story also is confused and rambling."

Daktar Akhter Hameed Khan (1914-1999): Poem in Urdu by Akbar Khan

Khala hai magar khali nahin phir bhi
Dil mein daktar sahib ka mission hai
Punam zaroor hain magar be-noor nahin
Aankhon mein meri unka vision hai

Yaad rahein gi ta hayaat baatein unki
Chori aur kamchori se kinara kashi
Apne liye to sab hi jeetay hain magar
Doosron keliye jeena hai asl zindagi

Wo doosron ke masail ko samjhna
Aur talaash karna unke hul
Kum lagat banana phir iss hul ko
Hai yehi action research ka amal

Wo logon ko samjhana ke apnay masail
Karo hul apni madad aap se
Kisi ke aagay na phailao haath
Bacho khairaat kay aazab se

Kaam ko apnay tum zarya banao
Zaat ko apni roz karnay ka bartar
Jo kal thay tum uss say dekhao
Thoraa saa aaj behtar bankar

Asal kaam dunya mein hai gar karna
Karo khoob tum logon ki khidmat
Zamin par pao gay tum izzat o shorat
Aur arshe bareen par tum jannat

Rahan ka tariqa rakho apna saada
Na numaish ho aur na dikhawa
Aik almari mein samajaey jo kuch bhi hai
Zaaid hai gar hai iss ke allaawa

Roshan kar gaye jo shammein Daktar Sahib

Ab hamara kaam hai unhein jalaey rakhna
Unki roshni ko suraj ke muqabil karna
Nazre bud se mukhalif hawaon se bachai rakhna

Goh jism saath nahin ruh to hamaray saath hai
Nek logon ka raha hai yehi asool
Jab bhi gheringi dunya ki wehshatein hamein
Hamari khatir hoga unka nazool

Akbar Khan
Karachi, October 11, 1999

Dr. Akhter Hameed Khan (1914-1999): Poem by Akbar Khan

Dr. Sahib has departed for his Heavenly Abode
But His mission lives on
Through his work, through us
His vision lives on

The lamps that he kindled
Will shine on forever
We resolve to carry his torch
In making others' lives better

His message of selfless service
Hard work, devotion, dedication
Caring for others above self
Sacrifice for the cause of nation

Competence and Honesty
He did always stress
Are sure-fire prerequisites
For eternal success

Lead a simple life
He would always say
Don't let materialism
Get in your way

Your job is just a tool
For personal development
Every day you must make
In your self – improvement

Dedicate your life
To the service of the needy
Attain contentment through service
Do not become greedy

Diagnose the problem

Plan out your solution
Implement your plan through
Action Research and demonstration

Build your models well
Technically sure and sound
The world will come to you
When no answers are to be found

In times of trouble
When darkness rules the day
Build a 'khanqah' of light
To show the way

Do not steal – it is 'chori'
Do not shirk – it is 'kamchori'
With competence and honesty
Achieve honor and glory

Admit your mistakes
Document them – do not hide
Carry on your efforts with
Renewed zeal and pride

Akbar Khan
Karachi, Pakistan
October 13, 1999

Photographs

Dr. Akhtar Hameed Khan delivering a speech in
East Pakistan (now Bangladesh)

Right to left: Shoaib Sultan Khan (winner of many prestigious
awards), Dr. Akhtar Hameed Khan, Dr. Rashid Bajwa (Chief
Executive Officer of National Rural Support Programme)

Right to left: Dr. Akhtar Hameed Khan, President of Pakistan
Muhammad Ayub Khan, Governor of East Pakistan
Abdul Monem Khan

Akhter Hameed Khan (2nd from left) with his brothers

Symposium in Islamabad (March 4-5, 2000)
Left to right: Arif Hasan, Shafiq Khan (Dr. Khan's second wife),
President Pervez Musharraf, Shoaib Sultan Khan,
A.T.M Shamsul Haq

Dr. Khan listening to a question from a gentleman

President of Bangladesh Hussain Mohammad Ershad presenting a plaque to Dr. Akhtar Hameed Khan

Left to right: Dr. Akhtar Hameed Khan and General Muhammad Musa Khan

Prime Minister of Pakistan Shaukat Aziz (then Finance Minister) speaking at the Dr. Akhtar Hameed Khan Memorial Lecture Sitting from left to right: Ozair A. Hanafi, Shoaib Sultan Khan (Chairman National Rural Support Program, NRSP), President of Khushali Bank, Ghalib Nishtar

Dr. Nasim Ashraf (then Chairman of the National Commission for Human Development (Pakistan) and Minister of State) and others attending Dr. Akhtar Hameed Khan Memorial Lecture

Dr. Akhtar Hameed Khan (2nd from left) and
Air Marshal Nur Khan (4th on right)

Lieutenant General Wajid Ali Khan with Dr. Akhtar Hameed Khan

Javed Jabbar (then Federal Minister for Information and Media
Development, sitting 3rd from left) and others at a
Memorial Seminar held in Karachi in honor of
Dr. Khan on October 31, 2001

The Memorial Seminar, attended by various dignitaries including
Omar Asghar Khan (Federal Minister for the Environment, Local
Government and Rural Development), Finance Minister Dr. Hafiz
Sheikh (then Minister of Finance, Government of Sindh, front row
extreme left), Dr. Sh. Tanveer, and Professor Ejaz Qureshi

Professor Richard O. Niehoff (Michigan State University)
with Dr. A.H. Khan

Article on Dr. Khan:
"Akhtar Hameed Khan and the Magic of Orangi"
Dawn (Pakistani newspaper) October 13, 1999

CROSSCURRENTS

The legendary Gandhian

Akhtar Hameed Khan, is remembered, on his first death anniversary, for his achievements in the field of urban management

ANIL AGARWAL AND SUNITA NARAIN

Just whom would you vote for as the greatest Gandhian in the Indian sub-continent of the post-Independence era? Our vote will unhesitatingly go to the Pakistani social scientist Akhtar Hameed Khan, in whose memory social activists from all over Pakistan met on October 12, 2000, his first death anniversary

and environmentally friendly as possible, the process of urbanisation has to be carefully managed in our part of the world. But urban systems, even in so-called democratic countries, are managed through mega-institutions, with elected representatives at the helm, at best. Instead of the urban institutional base being built on the rule of participatory democracy', it has been built on the rule of represen

Article on Dr. Khan:
"The Legendary Gandhian"
Down To Earth (Indian magazine) December 15, 2002

that the senior executives of the   stocks at substantial losses.

The death of a legend

IN THE death of Dr Akhter Hameed Khan, Pakistan has lost its greatest social scientist and humanitarian who became a legend in his lifetime. He was synonymous with the Orangi Pilot Project where his ideas, initiatives and inspiring leadership helped transform the lives of people in what was then called the biggest kachchi abadi of Asia. Though Orangi epitomized Dr Akhter Hameed's concept of community development through self-help, his humanitarian concern extended far beyond this settlement of 1.1 million on the outskirts of Karachi. As a social thinker and scholar, his influence was tremendous and was acclaimed internationally. He developed the research and the method of extension of his work — which involved low-profile research in community development on the ground — to evolve a strategy that was then applied in practice to transform the lives of people. His intellect and services won him the prestigious Magsaysay Award, he being the first Pakistani to have won it, and an honorary doctorate from the Michigan State University.

Striking deep roots in the communities with which he worked — be it the Comilla Rural Academy or the Orangi Pilot Project — Akhter Hameed Khan developed his ideas at the grassroots level. He was a genuine friend and benefactor of the neo

with the customs, traditions, likes and dislikes of the people. His profound understanding of the sociological, economic and political dimensions of life led him to two fundamental conclusions which formed the pivot of his social philosophy. His first finding was that people, who have been uprooted, will always seek to re-establish a sense of belonging, community feeling and ways of mutual help and cooperative action. His second observation was that the problems which people sought to solve foremost were those of housing, health care, education and employment. That is why these were the OPP's priorities wherein lay the key to its success.

A very modest and humane person, Dr Akhter Hameed Khan preferred not to claim any credit for the success of his projects. But the fact is that without his insightful guidance and the motivation and inspiration that he provided to the social activists and his dedicated band of followers, he could never have transformed the lives of the people he worked with. He had two basic qualities which marked his approach and ensured its success. First was his immense love for his people. A member of the prestigious ICS, he left that service a few years after joining it because he felt he could not solve the problems of the people from that position. He went to work as

Editorial on Dr. Khan:
"The Death of a Legend"
Dawn (Pakistani newspaper) October 12, 1999

TRIBUTE

Mighty in deed

On the occasion of his first death anniversary on October 12, social scientists from all over Pakistan gathered to honour the memory of one of the sub-continent's greatest Gandhians – Akhtar Hameed Khan.

ANIL AGARWAL and SUNITA NARAIN write on his achievements in the field of urban management. He will be especially remembered for his involvement with the Orangi Pilot Project in Karachi, where he mobilised the residents of this illegal squatter settlement, to finance and construct their own sanitation system.

Tribute to Dr. Akhtar Hameed Khan:
"Mighty in Deed"
The Hindu (daily from India) October 22, 2000

PIONEERS IN MICROFINANCE

Dr. Akhtar Hameed Khan is the originator of two development exemplars: the Comilla Model and the Orangi Pilot Project.

This series recognizing early innovators in social finance is generously underwritten by:

Deutsche Bank

Dr. Akhtar Hameed Khan

We diverge from our interview format this month to bring you the following profile of Dr. Khan, who passed away in 1999.

Dr. Akhtar Hameed Khan helped lay the basic foundations of the microcredit movement through his work on the Comilla Model of rural development in the 1960s and the Orangi Pilot Project in the 1980s. The Comilla Model, originally developed at the Bangladesh Academy of Rural Development (BARD), focused on the integration of public and private resources to create a collaborative institutional base for development work. The Orangi Pilot Project was initiated as a grassroots development project that emphasized self-help as the primary means of developing the "kacchi abadis" (informal sector).

Dr. Khan was born in 1914 in Agra, located in the state of Uttar Pradesh, India. He began his career in the prestigious Indian Civil Service in 1936, serving primarily in East Bengal and later pursuing to study literature at the University of Cambridge. Disillusioned after the Bengal Famine of 1943, he resigned from the Indian Civil Service to work as a locksmith. This was a very unusual choice for someone who had held such a coveted position. Historian Nasim Yousaf explains that Dr. Khan "wanted to study the poor man's life."

In the early 1950s, Dr. Khan returned to East Bengal, now Bangladesh, where he worked as the principal of Comilla Victoria College and became director of the newly formed BARD, where he developed the Comilla Model.

The Comilla Model is a rural development approach that evolved from a

After Bangladesh's independence in 1971, Dr. Khan served as a research fellow, visiting professor and advisor at several universities in Bangladesh, Pakistan and the United States. In 1980, he returned to Pakistan to continue grassroots development work through the Orangi Pilot Project, OPP, which emphasized self-help as the solution to obtaining capital and improving sanitation, health, education and employment within low-income settlements near Karachi. OPP assisted residents in family planning, improving construction, organized immunizations and helped install low-cost sewers that served 72,000 homes and 600,000 people at one-tenth the cost of conventional sewage systems.

> *He learned a lot when he was working as a locksmith, as a laborer.... He thought that people can be extremely productive...provided that they are organized somehow....*
>
> NASIM YOUSAF, HISTORIAN

A tribute to Dr. Akhtar Hameed by MicroCapital (USA), a monthly digest of microfinance

Index